Acclaim for
The View from
Paul's Window

Jeanie Shaw takes on a formidable task in her study of women in the New Testament. This does not mean that she rushes in where angels fear to tread. Many Christians in many quarters have engaged in this great dialogue, and this book provides a brave launch for that discussion as Jeanie's inquisitive spirit guides us readers toward profitable conversation. We both appreciate her kingdom perspective, biblical humility, and surrender to God's will. She tackles difficult passages with care and depth; however, her study remains accessible for all of us. Finally, her wit and affable prose keep you engaged from the first page to the last.
—Ed and Deb Anton, evangelist and women's ministry leader; Virginia Beach, Virginia

The cultural milieu in our day is so very different from that of the Roman Empire in the times of Jesus and Paul. That point was dramatically made recently when Lt. Gen. Laura J. Richardson became the first woman to lead the US Army Forces Command, or FORSCOM. She is now the commander of the largest command in the US military, representing 776,000 soldiers and 96,000 civilians.

In her book, The View from Paul's Window, *Jeanie Shaw looks out on a social and cultural landscape in the first century where such a development could not have been conceived. With a unique, but an extremely essential combination of conviction and humility, Jeanie calls us to reread certain biblical texts so we might hear afresh the heart of Jesus' message and not be bound or limited by a culture that existed sixty years ago or two thousand years ago. With a gentle and respectful method (she is no iconoclast), reinforced by careful scholarship, Jeanie raises questions that need to be raised and points us in helpful directions. Without a hint of a rebellious or resentful spirit, she gives us some new perspectives that enable us to think in fresh ways about the role of women in the Body of Christ.*

Jesus and Paul both liberated women in their day and they felt that. However, I am convinced that if we ignore voices like Jeanie's, we will greatly damage our efforts to bring the good news to at least over half the people in our world. But more importantly, we may lock down on a certain way of

coming to Scripture that will keep us from growing in other areas as well. Jeanie has written a courageous and timely book and we have much to gain by giving it prayerful consideration. I highly commend it.
—Tom Jones, author of numerous books; teacher; founder and former editor of DPI; Nashville, Tennessee

There has been a need for some time in our family of churches to have a substantive discussion on the role of women in the church and how to best read the pertinent New Testament passages. Jeanie has stepped into the gap and begun that discussion. She carefully looks back at the cultural and historical context surrounding the New Testament times in order to consider how having a firm grip on those realities might direct our interpretation and application of Scripture today. The View from Paul's Window is engaging and accessible to any reader, whether they have studied this topic before or are new to it. Every disciple should engage with this book and wrestle with the topics that Jeanie clearly and succinctly tackles. Whether you agree with her conclusions or not, I believe you will do well to be challenged by her points and engage in the conversation.
—Michael Burns, teaching minister; author of Crossing the Line: Culture, Race, and Kingdom; Minneapolis-St. Paul, Minnesota.

This is such an important book! It's so readable and so relevant to questions that are increasingly arising. Thank you so much for your work on this. I can't wait for it to be on my bookshelf!
—Linda Brumley, elder's wife; author; San Diego, California.

I loved what Jeanie had to say. It was very freeing and helped me to see the scriptures with new eyes. Her insights were incredible. This subject has been on my heart for a while, and I have been reading and listening to all kinds of podcasts. I have three daughters who are all very different but strong women. I enjoyed the insightful way Jeanie started with hermeneutics and exegesis, then went into the concept of slavery. I appreciate all the ways she touched on different issues like wearing hats or no hats, submission in marriage, leadership out of humility, etc. It was all wonderfully enlightening I appreciate the ways she expresses her thoughts and opinions in this book. She did not come across like she had the final truth. I am so grateful for the time and energy she took to deeply study this subject and to

write this book. I and many sisters will be forever appreciative.
—Erica Kim, elder's wife; author; Denver, Colorado.

I've always loved and admired Jeanie's creativity.... and now I'm extra thankful for her curiosity and stubbornness—and the way those characteristics moved her to study this topic and wrestle with her background (which is similar to mine)! The fact that this is such a challenging topic didn't deter her from taking it on, and I applaud her for taking on such a task! Jeanie's spirit in this book is great—she makes it very clear that there are many opinions on these issues, and that she is not trying to give a "final word." I appreciate her coming back to Paul's heart to be like Jesus, in wanting as many men and women as possible to be saved. This thought was helpful for me. I gained a better understanding of many cultural concepts and practices, and I appreciate her for doing the research to show the ways background and culture played such a part in what Paul needed to address.

I pray that we women may continue to work with our men to influence our families to be lights for the world, to his glory!
—Gloria Baird, elder's wife; author; Paradise. (Gloria wrote these words shortly before she passed away in July, 2018.)

I find it interesting that we as a fellowship of churches have continued to adapt our practices both consciously and unconsciously. Women were hired to be "in the ministry" fairly early on but were limited in ways that Jeanie mentions. A couple of decades ago, we discussed and accepted the ideas of women baptizing women, women serving as ushers and passers of communion trays, and women sharing thoughts along with their husbands in communion talks.

Gradually we began to accept more public types of participation. Married couples taught together about marriage and parenting principles, and at times men and women have taught together on various other topics. We may have prefaced such team teaching with the statements that the women were addressing women, but the men didn't insert earplugs when the women were teaching, and I was often as convicted and inspired by what the women taught as by the men's teaching (sometimes more so).

The question is whether we "drifted" into these changes or gradually adapted to the culture changes around us without violating scriptures. I tend to answer that it was the latter. Paul became all things to all people in order to save as many as possible. I want to do the same. I distinctly recall many instances as a younger person thinking that the older generations were old-fashioned and out of touch with reality. Our young people in the church often view us in the same way. I think that we were often accurate in our assessments—as are many in the younger generations today. Thus, I am more than willing to reconsider our views of the women's roles in the church as a part of being willing (anxious, actually) to become all things to all people in order to save as many as possible.

Whether we all end up in complete agreement or not (we won't), we will be enriched by further study and less likely to be entrenched in views that are more opinion than we previously thought.

—Gordon Ferguson, teacher; author of numerous books; McKinney, Texas.

I deeply appreciate Jeanie's study and research (which I'm sure was excruciating at times). To write a book on this topic requires an author who is extremely humble and dedicated to following God's word. Jeanie is that person. Many people have asked for a book like this; I'm grateful that The View From Paul's Window can provide so many helpful insights to those who want to consider this complicated but timely subject.

—Kay McKean, retired women's ministry leader; author; Maui, Hawaii.

Jeanie Shaw shares with her readers a stimulating study of the issues surrounding women and authority. Given the wealth of material in circulation, as well as the diversity of viewpoints, such a task requires great patience and careful study. Shaw's study is not only thoughtful and well done—it's nuanced and interesting. She is to be commended, and this volume welcomed.

—Douglas Jacoby, teacher; author; Adjunct Professor of Bible and Theology, Lincoln Christian University; Atlanta, Georgia.

The View from Paul's Window is well-structured and thoughtful. Jeanie Shaw's writing style is approachable and humble. I appreciated the many personal notes she included, which allow readers to get a sense of who she is and her motivation for tackling these questions. Jeanie's explanation of the historical-cultural context for Paul's epistles is thorough and provides a plausible interpretation for the potentially negative commands in the texts regarding women. The last couple of chapters bring out potential applications for congregations today.

—Dr. Melinda (Mindi) Thompson, Associate Professor of Bible, Abilene Christian University Graduate School of Theology; Abilene, Texas

In her book The View from Paul's Window Jeanie Shaw has created a deeply personal and inspiring work. Jeanie courageously tackles the age-old (and often controversial) topic of women's roles in the church. In this case she does it through the eyes of the Apostle Paul. Because Jeanie writes from the heart, what is revealed is her passion for this topic—along with her many years of ministry experience and leadership that back her points of view. While not intended to be exhaustive in its scope, Jeanie turns to excellent source materials in providing her audience with perspectives that will spark each reader to think deeper and more seriously about God's intentions for the women in our spiritual community. I have no doubt that this book will inspire readers to dive into further research in the scriptures and to pray for the guidance of the Holy Spirit in gaining wisdom in the areas Jeanie tackles here. I applaud Jeanie's courage and hard work to open the dialogue concerning our beloved sisters in our fellowship.

—Phil Lasarsky, teacher; Chicago, Illinois.

I deeply admire Jeanie's humility, courage, and the loving labor invested in service to all of us as she produced this book. I believe we need the principles and information she presents here in order to do the best job we can of preparing and inspiring women in our churches for works of service (Eph 4:12).

—Tammy Fleming, author and missionary; Kiev, Ukraine

In early 2017, the Midwest teachers were tasked by regional evangelists to tackle the subject of the role of women; this was about the same time that Jeanie Shaw was already immersed in her own study. My primary role on the team was to record and report on the process itself. When Jeanie sent us an early draft of The View from Paul's Window, we observed that most of the collective judgements of our cross-disciplinary teacher's group were in the same ballpark as Jeanie's perspectives, or vice-versa.

It is my opinion that the ever-so-conscientious Jeanie Shaw has provided a splendid and reasonable aid to help others flesh out important issues, opportunities, and boundaries.

—Steve Staten, teacher; organizational health consultant; Chicago, Illinois

I have been eager for this book to be published so I can use it in our mission school in the SPA region. Thank you, Jeanie, for writing this needed book.

—Teresa Fontenot, women's ministry leader; elder's wife; Sydney, Australia

A discussion on the topic of women's role in the church is, I believe, much needed in our fellowship of churches today. Disciples want to know the biblical guidelines for women (and men) in the church. The answer to this question revolves around whether or not one sees the passages in the Bible which speak to this issue as cultural or normative for today. Jeanie Shaw has attempted to address this issue in her book The View from Paul's Window. Whether or not one agrees with everything she says (indeed no one agrees with everything anyone writes, and I do have some points in her book that I disagree with as well), I believe she has done excellent research and delineated the issues well. She is fair and balanced, not dogmatic in any way. I see humility on every page. Her book is, I think, a great starting point for discussion of this crucial issue for the church today, no matter which side of the issue one's convictions presently fall.

—Glenn Giles, PhD, Adjunct Professor of Bible at Lincoln Christian University and Director and Professor of Bible and Theology at Rocky Mountain School of Ministry and Theology; Denver, Colorado.

In today's volatile socio-political climate, Christians are in desperate need of good kindling for meaningful dialogue on the pressing issues of our day. One of the red-hot topics we are being confronted with regards how we, as a global society, relate to women. Jeanie Shaw's book The View from Paul's Window: Paul's Teaching on Women is a welcome spark for discussions on what the Bible and Paul really mean to say about women.

The terminology of meaning has been employed in recent history to justify taking political and religious positions based on immediate cultural imperatives. Oftentimes these imperatives are not motivated by faithfulness to an orthodox reading of Scripture. So when we start trying to venture down this road, we can be blamed of cleverly shifting the conversations with some hermeneutical trickery.

In contrast, I have found this book to be an honest, open, orthodox, and probing search into the Apostle Paul's writings in the New Testament regarding women. This is the location of the Bible's most controversial statements about women's place in the Christian community. Paul's statements have been an interpretive enigma for some time. Jeanie has thoroughly and effectively unpacked the topic with a scholarly seriousness, but her writing is also very accessible. It should be a welcome tool for people of every reading level.

I received this book with great anticipation because I have felt the burden and deep need to engage in a renewed discussion about scripture and women. I truly believe this book is an answer to many people's prayers and needs. I have found The View from Paul's Window to be a refreshingly biblical and orthodox engagement with scripture on a topic pressing for a fresh reading.

It is my hope that every Christian will read this book, taking some time to reevaluate, rethink, renew, and refresh the way they read scripture. When it comes down to it, this is what we are being encouraged to do: Take the Bible back into our hands and faithfully read it with tools such as the ones Jeanie has offered to be put into our tool belt. I believe this will help us to see the topic of women in scripture in a new light. We will be able to have a great sense of confidence as we employ these tools to engage family, friends, coworkers, and community on this vitally important topic.

—James Becknell, minister and teacher; Chicago, Illinois.

The View from Paul's Window is very well written. I enjoyed reading it. It is thoughtful, and the arguments are made clearly. The method of writing easily takes the reader from one point to another.

This is a much-needed book on a subject of grand importance. I have always felt that sisters were unjustly kept from expressing their gifts because of passages of scriptures that were misinterpreted and misunderstood. I think that this book can go a long way to help sisters use and express their God given talents and gifts.

This is not just a book to casually read, such as a blog or other type of similar article. This is a book to challenge the very belief systems of many people, especially brothers, into more clearly thinking about the role of women.

I have had to really meditate on some of the principles Jeanie has stated in her book. I thought I had understood the question of what a sister can and cannot do with respect to brothers, but now I am not so sure.

The vast amount of information she provides on women in the scriptures was eye-opening. Although I have read the stories over various times, putting the passages into perspective as to how much Jesus actually did rely upon women in his ministry and how he used them in examples made me stop and think.

—Dan Demshar, elder and teacher; Boston, Massachusetts.

The View from Paul's Window:
Paul's Teachings on Women

Jeanie Shaw

The View from Paul's Window: Paul's Teachings on Women
Copyright © 2020 by Jeanie Shaw

ISBN: 9781948450249.

Published by Illumination Publishers, 6010 Pinecreek Ridge Court, Spring, Texas 77379, (www.ipibooks.com).

All rights reserved. No part of this publication may be reproduced, stored in a retrieval system, or transmitted in any form or by any means—electronic, mechanical, digital, photocopy, recording,or any other—except for brief quotations in printed reviews, without the prior permission of the author and publisher.

Illumination Publishers titles may be purchased in bulk for classroom instruction, business, fund-raising, or sales promotional use. For information, please e-mail paul at paul.ipibooks@me.com.

All Scripture quotations, unless otherwise indicated, are from The Holy Bible, New International Version. Copyright © 1973, 1978, 1984, 2011 by Biblica, Inc. Used by permission. All rights reserved worldwide.

All Scriptures marked NLT are from the *Holy Bible, New Living Translation*. Copyright © 1996, 2004, 2007 by Tyndale House Foundation. Used by permission.

Text layout by Toney Mulhollan and cover design by Roy Appalsamy.

Appendix C is taken from the Foreword by Jerry Taylor, "Jeanene Showed Up and God Showed Out," in *Bound and Determined: Christian Men and Women in Partnership* by Jeanene Reese (Leafwood Publishers, 2010). Used by permission of the publisher. All Rights reserved.

About the author: Jeanie Shaw has served in the ministry for forty-six years. She has taught classes and workshops on various topics in many countries and has authored fourteen books. She has her master's degree in Christian Spirituality and Formation and is pursuing her doctorate in the same field. Jeanie was married for forty-five years and has four adult children and eight grandchildren. Keep up with Jeanie at her website: www.jeaniesjourneys.com.

Author update: After I wrote this book over two-and-a-half years ago, several significant events happened. My beloved husband, who is mentioned in the present tense in some of the pages in this book went to be with the Lord on November 21, 2019. He challenged and inspired me to have courage throughout this project, and both his love and words of wisdom accompany me every day.

Also, in January 2020, several teachers in my church fellowship produced a scholarly work on many New Testament passages entitled *The Bible and Gender*, which is referenced in the bibliography.

Jeanie Shaw, July 2020

Contents

Acknowledgments ... 13
Foreword ... 15
Introduction ... 17

Part 1: Digging into Scripture

Chapter 1: Meeting Exo-Jesus and Herman Newticks ... 27
Chapter 2: Culture Matters: The Garden Culture and Redemption's Counterculture ... 39
Chapter 3: Paul's Window Seat ... 49
Chapter 4: The New Woman: The Burning of the ~~Bras~~ Veils ... 55
Chapter 5: Church Culture in Corinth and Ephesus ... 65
Chapter 6: Addressing Dressing: You Were What You Wore ... 71
Chapter 7: Soap Opera or Scripture? Childbirth, Widows, Deception, Silence, Authority, and Order ... 85
Chapter 8: How Silent Is Silence? ... 93

Part 2: Aiming Toward Progress in Partnerships

Chapter 9: Partnership and Unity in Ephesians Five ... 107
Chapter 10: Embracing Paradoxes ... 121
Chapter 11: Women as Fellow Workers ... 133
Appendix A: American Chattel Slavery as Compared to Ancient Greco-Roman Slavery ... 147
Appendix B: Historical Highlights and Lowlights of Women: From Paul's Day Through the Restoration Movement ... 149
Appendix C: New Wineskins Retreat: A Powerful Example of Inclusion ... 159
Endnotes ... 163
Bibliography ... 173

Acknowledgments

When a book is born, the author is often left exhausted. Writing a book resembles (to me) a birthing process. The entire process takes time. (And I could have birthed an overdue elephant with the years it took me to complete this book!) The birth process includes a gestation period and maturation process, often accompanied by complications like tiredness, nausea, and overactive emotions. The culmination is both painful and exhilarating.

Thankfully, knowledgeable doctors, nurses, and midwives, along with encouraging coaches, friends, and family members, can surround us to make the process better.

These attendants helped me birth this book. Thank you. Doctors and nurses (the academics) assisted me by checking facts, anachronisms, Biblical languages details, and by contributing valuable information. Thanks to Michael Burns for his helpful details on slavery and for giving me the idea for the arrow analogy; Steve Kinnard, DMin, for his support and thoughtful foreword, Douglas Jacoby, DMin, for checking facts and offering suggestions; Phil Lasarsky for sharing from his studies in the Old Testament and for sharing Hebrew meanings of words; Gordon Ferguson, a Bible teacher, for spending many hours with me discussing topics covered in the book, and for offering input for better structure and approach; Dan Demshar, a Biblical languages scholar who spent his lunch hour for months checking details and offering insight; Lory Demshar who offered valuable suggestions; James Becknell for his contributions on the Restoration period; Professor Melinda Thompson (Abilene Christian University) for taking the time to read and give thoughts on exegesis; Matina Montes for consistent encouragement and feedback, and for leading me to valuable resources; Dr. Deb Anton and Teresa Fontenot, whose classes helped me jump off the starting block to begin this book; Jason Alexander, Jeremy Lefler, Steve Staten, Glenn Giles, ThD, PhD, and Tammy Fleming, who took time to read and provide thoughtful input. Thank you.

My "midwives and coaches" have been invaluable. Elizabeth Thompson, my gifted editor, continually offers wise counsel, correction, expertise, laughter, and support—making this book much better (and at times talking me off the ledge). Kay McKean has been a constant encouragement in this process, as has Erica Kim and Kim Evans. Gloria Baird and Linda Brumley also took time to read and provide feedback, encouragement and kind "blurbs." Thank you.

My friends are a great source of encouragement to me when I write. Your support means more to me than you can ever know.

My daughters (true ezers) inspire me and spur me on, and my sons know how to strengthen me and keep me laughing. Finally, and most importantly, I want to thank my husband, Wyndham, for living the example of one who loves his wife as Christ loves the church, for supporting me (even when the subject matter is a little unnerving), for listening to me read draft after draft, and for putting up with me during nights when my light is on much too late. There are no words to adequately express my love and appreciation for you, my greatest supporter and fan. Even though, because of your illness, you can no longer do the things you were once able to do, you continue to do what's most important. You love like Jesus. Thank you.

Foreword

Spiritual women have always provided inspirational leadership for God's people. Think of the prophet Miriam, the judge Deborah, the social justice activist Rizpah, the prophet Huldah, Queen Esther, Mary the mother of Jesus, Mary the disciple of Jesus, the anonymous women who supported the ministry of Jesus, the prophets known as the four daughters of Philip, Tabitha, Phoebe, Pricilla, and the list goes on.

Do you remember the prophet Anna in Luke 2? Anna was a prophet who waited in the temple of Jerusalem every day for the arrival of the Messiah. She fasted and prayed for his appearance. When she met the child Jesus, she was filled with gratitude and went throughout the temple sharing her discovery with people who were waiting for the redemption of Israel. Anna was an eighty-four year old single woman, a widow, who used her gift of prophecy to announce the arrival of the Messiah. Anna was one of many spiritual women in the Bible who inspired God's people.

I wonder how the prophet Anna would be received in our churches today? I wonder how her gift would be used in our churches? If you read Jeanie Shaw's book, *The View from Paul's Window: Paul's Teachings on Women,* then you'll see that Jeanie is asking the same questions. Jeanie exegetes all the major passages where Paul teaches about women, and then she draws meaning from these passages for our churches today.

The time has arrived for disciples of Jesus to discuss the most effective path to insure that women in the church can develop and use their spiritual gifts for God's glory. *The View from Paul's Window: Paul's Teachings on Women* lays a foundation for this discussion.

Jeanie tackles tough topics in her book—topics like biblical exegesis, principles of interpretation, the use of head coverings, submission and authority, the permissibility of women to teach men, deaconesses, etc. She approaches these topics head on and doesn't shrink away from the knowledge that not everyone will agree with her conclusions. There are points in the book where Jeanie admits, "This is my opinion." All good theological writing includes such an admission. As you read the book, you understand that her opinion is an informed one which is supported by hours and hours of scholarly research, contemplation, and discussion.

Jeanie isn't dogmatic about her conclusions. She gives her informed opinions, but leaves room for discussion. She also acknowledges that we must translate our understanding of the text to various cultures around the world. What we practice as churches in the United States may not look the same as what churches in the Middle East practice. That's okay.

I'm grateful to Jeanie for her book. Her research on this topic is evident on every page she has written. Taking on these passages is not an easy task. By writing this book, Jeanie has provided a great service for our movement.

I read dozens of books every year. I never agree with everything an author writes. In fact, I no longer agree with everything I wrote thirty years ago. We learn as we grow, and we grow as we learn.

I imagine that not every reader will agree with everything in Jeanie's book. That's okay. Producing books like *The View from Paul's Window* is how we make progress on topics where our opinions differ. I don't get the sense that Jeanie is looking for each reader to agree with her every opinion. I get a sense that she wants to launch an informed discussion on this topic. She has accomplished this in her book. This book serves as a launching pad for healthy dialogue on this crucial issue.

Some of you will think Jeanie has not gone far enough in her book to shatter the glass ceiling for women in church leadership. Others will say her opinions at certain points have gone too far. I'm grateful that she has moved the ball down the field. I'm grateful that she has started a conversation.

Now, let's talk.

—Dr. G. Steve Kinnard
Adjunct Professor of Bible, Lincoln Christian University
Dean of Ministry and Bible, Rocky Mountain School of Ministry and Theology

Introduction

Several years ago I was asked to speak on 1 Timothy 2:15 to a group of women at a Bible school in Europe. They wanted me to speak on the verse, "But women will be saved through childbearing—if they continue in faith, love and holiness with propriety."

I thought perhaps the organizers had sent me the wrong passage, but to my dismay, I had received the accurate assignment. How would I possibly speak on this passage? And if this scripture wasn't confusing enough, I considered the four previous verses:

> A woman should learn in quietness and full submission. I do not permit a woman to teach or to assume authority over a man; she must be quiet. For Adam was formed first, then Eve. And Adam was not the one deceived; it was the woman who was deceived and became a sinner. But women will be saved through childbearing—if they continue in faith, love and holiness with propriety. (1 Timothy 2:11–14 NIV)

Truthfully, I was scared of these passages and of this assignment. These verses were not among my favorites, so I had filed them away in my mental files under "confusing stuff." They seemed so odd, random, and difficult to understand. I maintained a simple explanation of "This is all cultural," but had no specific details to back up my explanation. So, I figured I had some studying to do to prepare for this assignment. While I was at it I added 1 Corinthians 11:3–16 and 1 Corinthians 14:29–35 to my study list, just to further complicate my mind with more of Paul's confusing writings.

> But I want you to realize that the head of every man is Christ, and the head of the woman is man, and the head of Christ is God. Every man who prays or prophesies with his head covered dishonors his head. But

every woman who prays or prophesies with her head uncovered dishonors her head—it is the same as having her head shaved. For if a woman does not cover her head, she might as well have her hair cut off; but if it is a disgrace for a woman to have her hair cut off or her head shaved, then she should cover her head.

A man ought not to cover his head, since he is the image and glory of God; but woman is the glory of man. For man did not come from woman, but woman from man; neither was man created for woman, but woman for man. It is for this reason that a woman ought to have authority over her own head, because of the angels. Nevertheless, in the Lord woman is not independent of man, nor is man independent of woman. For as woman came from man, so also man is born of woman. But everything comes from God.

Judge for yourselves: Is it proper for a woman to pray to God with her head uncovered? Does not the very nature of things teach you that if a man has long hair, it is a disgrace to him, but that if a woman has long hair, it is her glory? For long hair is given to her as a covering. If anyone wants to be contentious about this, we have no other practice—nor do the churches of God. (1 Corinthians 11:3–16 NIV)

Two or three prophets should speak, and the others should weigh carefully what is said. And if a revelation comes to someone who is sitting down, the first speaker should stop. For you can all prophesy in turn so that everyone may be instructed and encouraged. The spirits of prophets are subject to the control of prophets. For God is not a God of disorder but of peace—as in all the congregations of the Lord's people.

Women should remain silent in the churches. They are not allowed to speak, but must be in submission, as the law says. If they want to inquire about something, they should ask their own husbands at home; for it is disgraceful for a woman to speak in the church. (1 Corinthians 14:29–35 NIV)

These scriptures seemed to me to be as clear as mud!

As I studied I found nearly as many interpretations of these scriptures as there were books on the subject. Thoughts varied wildly, often arguing for completely opposing meanings. Most scholars consider these scriptures to be some of the most difficult New Testament passages to understand. (Actually, that makes me feel better.)

I'm extremely curious by nature, and I can also be stubborn. These qualities are sometimes helpful and sometimes detrimental, and

I continue to experience both outcomes as I live life. I have stayed up all night trying to learn how to install routers, fix my computer, repair my vacuum cleaner, find missing objects—and try to grasp Paul's intended meaning of "saved through childbirth." Thanks to my curiosity and stubbornness I did fix my computer, install the router (eventually), and repair the vacuum cleaner (sort of).

But the scriptural dilemmas...those weren't so quickly resolved. I had a few more sleep-deprived nights pondering the "childbirth" verse and Paul's other difficult writings about women. I kept rereading these scriptures, thinking perhaps I was missing something. I then recalled a fictitious story of an agnostic who suffered from insomnia and dyslexia and stayed up all night wondering if there was indeed a dog. Of course, this did not help. Back to more serious methods of scriptural study.

Over time I had conversations with more people who expressed similar confusion, and even disagreement, over these scriptures. Some women I know felt compelled to change their style of dress and begin wearing head coverings to church; other women from my congregation asked me why they could not teach to a coed audience; still other women told me they felt our fellowship of churches did not adequately use women's gifts. Millennials raised questions that stumped me. All this combined to pique my desire to learn the meaning of Paul's writings about women (there goes my curiosity), so I dove in, spending countless hours reading and learning as much as I could (and there goes my stubbornness).

While numerous scholars have researched these scriptures for years, they have not reached a common conclusion—far from it! Scholars argue for a wide range of interpretations and conclusions. Some interpret Paul's writings as applying primarily to the specific culture and needs of Paul's day, while others discount the role of culture and view Paul's instructions as holding transcultural authority for all Christians for all time. Others explore the nuances and meanings of significant words that may have been "lost in translation." If there were a conclusion clear enough to be accepted by all, we would not have such a variety of opinions and writings.

I decided that I could either keep ignoring the difficult scriptures—let them keep gathering dust in my "confusing stuff" file—or I could wholeheartedly attempt to discern Paul's intended message. I entered this study out of curiosity, confusion, and a sincere desire to seek truth, not because of some personal issue or agenda. I have no ax to grind. I feel fulfilled as a woman, I enjoy a wonderful marriage, and I feel respected by many men. In studying Paul's writings about women, I simply desired to find greater understanding.

As I studied, I felt challenged by my preconceived notions and assumptions as well as my incomplete knowledge of church history, ancient cultures, and language nuances that are helpful in clearly understanding scripture. I was also confronted with the ways my cultural and spiritual heritage has shaped what I do or don't do as a woman in God's church—at times without fully understanding the scriptural reasoning behind those choices.

I began to realize that as a woman, I harbored prejudices I did not know I held—a subtle "less than" attitude toward myself or other women as teachers. For example, numerous times I wanted to throw this manuscript in the fire, wondering, "What in the world am I thinking, attempting to write a book like this?" I theorized, "Writing on such a topic will certainly be seen as presumptuous—a man or scholar is certainly more qualified to write on such a subject." Although I began this study with no intention of writing a book, over time God put this book on my heart as I became increasingly invigorated in my study and writing.

Years ago I took part in a United Nations conference on Capitol Hill. I was representing needs of the poor in Eastern Europe with the hope of introducing policies that could be helpful to the underserved in that particular area of the world. As a "newbie" to the process and protocol of representing a nongovernmental organization, I remember having the same sense of "What am I doing here?" that I felt as I turned my studies into a book. I was unfamiliar with the political jargon of Capitol Hill and didn't know the names of "significant players" in the field. I was naïve to the whole scene; however I had spent many days with children and workers in orphanages in Eastern Europe and had tried to understand the plight of young teenagers living in the sewers. As I sat in the meeting, many high-sounding words and ideas for "fixing the problems" were expressed by the participants, which often seemed impractical and nonsensical to me. I decided to ask the group gathered there (sincerely wanting to know), how many of them had actually spent time in Eastern Europe. None of the participants had been there. None. And yet they confidently expounded on ways to assist the underprivileged of that area.

Likewise, as I began my study of Paul's teachings on women I did not know the definitions of words like *egalitarian* and *complementarian*, nor did I know the names of prominent scholars on the "debate scene." But I did have years of experience reading my Bible and functioning as a woman in the church. So, as I write about scriptures on women, I know that I have credibility as a woman and as a devoted disciple who has a passion for learning, reading, and teaching—but I don't claim to be a scholar. Most of my reading before this study had been exclusively based on the views and traditions in which I was raised.

I will also state from the beginning that I am not a feminist. A feminist is primarily concerned with defending and promoting women's rights. As a disciple of Jesus, I have learned that following him means laying down my rights—becoming more concerned with loving God and my neighbor than with protecting myself and my "rights." Unfortunately, at times I try to reclaim the rights I once laid down, as I like for things to be fair. However, life is not fair. It was not fair for Jesus, and it won't be fair for us. (As I will share later, I'm *glad* it's not fair. If it were, and if God treated me the way I deserve, I would have no hope for salvation!) I believe we can all grow in laying down our rights, loving God, and loving our neighbors. I know I certainly can grow in all of these areas. I pray that in some way this book will encourage humble conversations concerning ways we might work together more lovingly and effectively as male and female "neighbors" in the church today.

I have included in Appendix C a foreword to a book from a professor at Abilene Christian University. While the foreword is anecdotal and not a biblical study, the writer poignantly expresses the importance of understanding each other as we view scripture—and the refreshment that comes when we build unity and partnership through repentance and thoughtful conversation.

After spending several years praying and reading books, commentaries, and study tools, the scriptures began making more sense to me. My mind and heart were stretched as I sought to better understand Paul's teachings. I became more keenly aware of my own cultural background—the window through which I view the world. I challenged myself to think outside my familiar comfort zone. Over time, some of my thinking has changed and grown.

I am more grateful than ever for the value and purpose God has bestowed upon women. More grateful than ever for the beautiful equality given to men and women as demonstrated by Jesus and further instructed by Paul. I am confident that God gives women more avenues to receive and express our love for him than we have likely realized.

The pages of this book are intended to explore Paul's difficult passages on women. I intend to "take the bull by the horns" (or perhaps, because of the topic of this book, I shall also "take the heifer by the udder"). We will look at terminology and cultural background with the intent to step outside our own cultural boundaries and reconsider them. While my studies have shaped my personal understanding, each of us must wrestle with the scriptures and come to our own understandings and convictions, while treating those who have come to different understandings with full respect. I do not intend this book to be the final word on this subject, but rather a conversation starter.

Dr. Jeanene Reese, professor at Abilene Christian University, offered an observation worth considering:

> I am firmly convinced that the church, fully engaged with the prevailing culture, must lead the way in establishing and supporting godly partnerships between men and women. To do so requires that we have thoughtful conversation with Scripture and culture in order to know how to interact effectively with both. To do anything else is to ignore not only how we are shaped by culture, but also how we influence it.[1]

We all approach life—and scripture—from our own perspective, which is influenced by multiple factors: our upbringing, our experiences, our gender, our race, our heritage, our religion, our family background, our education, and so much more. All these elements combine to create the "window" through which we view the world. Two people can observe the same scene from two different windows and come away with entirely different views. Our windows are often fogged with our own cultural and traditional biases.

I remember a time early in my ministry (in the early 1980s) when I was studying the Bible with my neighbor, who was eager to become a Christian. One day when I went over to visit she opened her refrigerator, revealing a six-pack of beer. I explained to her that if she were to become a Christian she would need to stop drinking alcohol. Although my friend was willing to change anything God commanded in order to become a Christian, she told me, "I know I need to change my thinking to conform to God's thinking, but can you show me some scriptures about that? I need to be sure God really thinks I need to give up alcohol."

In my Christian walk I had always tried to function "by the rules," and thanks to my Southern fundamentalist background, I had always been taught that drinking alcohol was a sin. I did not even want to walk past liquor stores in case someone saw me and thought I had gone inside the store. In my mind, if a Christian were to be seen coming out of a liquor store, that person would be viewed as a hypocrite and fraud.

But as I studied with my friend, I realized that my thinking had been based on tradition more than scripture. I confessed that I could find no scripture in the Bible proclaiming that drinking beer was wrong. The only sinful behaviors in the Bible concerning alcohol were drunkenness or being mastered by anything other than God. In fact, as I searched the scriptures, I learned that Paul had instructed Timothy to drink wine to help his stomach issues. And I'm fairly certain the disciples in Corinth weren't getting drunk on Welch's grape juice when they observed the Lord's Supper—the church was serving wine at their gatherings (see 1 Corinthians 11:20–21). Although this example may seem silly to you, it was a wake-up call to me, helping to illuminate what power my culture and background held over my study of the Bible. I became more aware that, moving forward, I needed to allow my Bible study to correct biases I carried from my own cultural background. It is likely that we all carry far more cultural biases than we imagine.

In the coming pages I pray we can gain a deeper insight into Paul's teachings on women, better understand his purposes for writing, and better discern how his instructions may or may not apply to us today.

If you are looking for an absolute, clear answer to every question for which Paul's writing begs answers, you will be disappointed with this book. If, however, you want valuable information that allows you to consider Paul's words with greater understanding, I hope you will find this book a helpful guide. These chapters contain my opinions from my study, not a statement of belief or practice for any church. I pray that this presentation of thoughts on Paul's teachings derived from my study will be useful for your own study, prayer, and humble, respectful conversations. This is my intent.

While much of the content of this book is informational, I have tried to assemble it in a readable and practical way. Part 1 includes chapters that attempt to explore Paul's meaning in his "difficult to understand" passages on women. Part 2 is an attempt to discuss more pragmatic ways we might apply these scriptures to our situations. My prayer is that this compilation will leave you with greater understanding of and admiration for the heart of Jesus as reflected through his servant Paul—a man who, like Jesus, longs for all men and women to be saved.

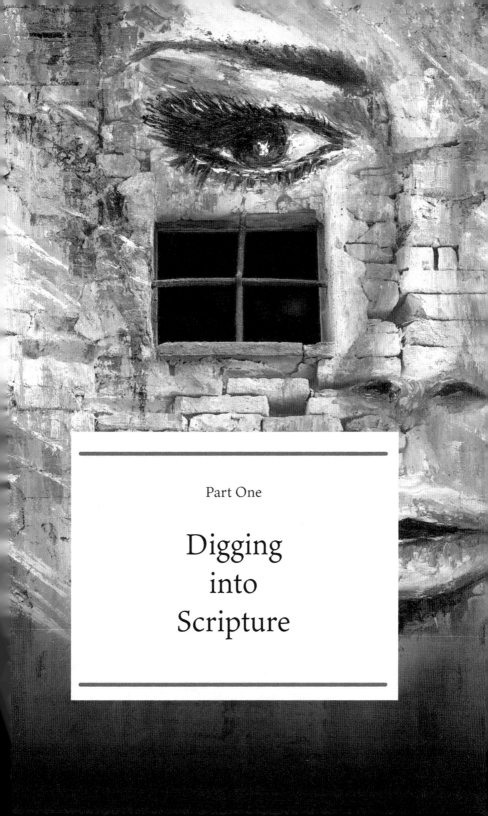

Part One

Digging into Scripture

Meeting Exo-Jesus and Herman Newticks

Before we dive deep into the topic of women's roles, we must establish some ground rules. To establish those ground rules, we need to define two important terms: exegesis and hermeneutics.

Although I grew up going to church three times a week and reading the Bible most every day, I had never heard of exegesis and hermeneutics. I first heard the terms when my husband went to graduate school. As I heard the word *exegesis* (which I always think sounds more like "Exo-Jesus" when spoken with a Southern accent), I wondered what this word meant, and assumed it had something to do with the external, physical Jesus (as in, his exoskeleton). Furthermore, I had never heard of Herman Newticks, but assumed he was some well-known scholar in academia. (The first example is true. The second is slightly exaggerated, though I did wonder about the weirdness of the word!)

These terms are important to understand in order to comprehend Paul's perspective as he viewed life—and wrote letters—from his window.

Exegesis, simply defined, is the use of critical analysis of scripture in order to discover its original meaning. Exegesis analyzes the literary and cultural context of scriptures with the end goal of answering the question: What did the original writer intend and what would the original reader have understood? *Exegesis* comes from a Greek word meaning "to draw out of." It is the opposite of *eisegesis,* which is to "read into" a text from our own biases and contexts. Proper exegesis occurs when we seek to discover the author's intended meaning, freeing it from our own personal and cultural biases.

Although we would all agree that the principle of exegesis is very important, it is sometimes inconsistently applied to the biblical passages addressing the role of women. A writer, speaker, or teacher may claim that one verse is inapplicable today because it is a command rooted in an ancient culture, but then declare that the very next verse is a teaching that transcends time and culture and is applicable for all times and places.

In this book we will attempt to identify some ground rules for reading and applying scripture. Which scriptures apply to God's people in every generation and culture, and which passages were intended to address a problem in a specific time among a particular people—and how do we make such a determination? Some commands did seem to have an "expiration date" in the sense that they could not or should not be applied eternally. (For example, when Jesus declared all foods clean [see Mark 7:19 and Acts 10:9–16], his declaration overwrote the Old Testament food laws.) But we must make such judgments with great care and study. If we conclude that any teaching from the scriptures no longer applies to us today, our reasoning needs to be both clear and accurate, because we are dealing with God's Word. If we want to perform exegesis on Paul's writings, we must pay close attention to the ground rules we establish.

Throughout this book we will explore questions raised from Paul's writings, including:

- What does Paul mean when he talks about head coverings?
- What does "headship" (a figurative description of someone at the top of a chain of command) mean in a marriage?
- Can a woman teach a coed class or workshop, or lead a coed worship team in the church?
- Can a woman speak in the public assembly?
- What does it mean for a woman to usurp authority?
- What does it mean to use the gifts we have been given?
- Does the chronology of creation have anything to do with hierarchy?

Easy topics, right?

I realize this book—and my take on some of these topics—will seem controversial to some readers and yet seem "wimpy" to others. For this reason, as well as my own desire to learn and grow, I have not written this book in a vacuum. I have asked numerous other people, all with expertise and strong knowledge of the Bible, to check my facts and give me feedback. It's been a great learning experience that has brought me to deeper convictions and fuller understanding.

I realize the thoughts I have written are my opinions, and not everyone will agree with me. On some topics I express clear conclusions, but on other topics the best I can offer is a "leaning"—my best guess as to the proper interpretation. If we are not completely sure of our conclusions, even if we lean strongly in a certain direction, and the matter is not a salvation issue, we should probably consider the topic a "disputable matter." With that in mind, I share a thought from Gordon Ferguson, from his book on Romans:

> The differences here are in the realm of opinion, to be sure, but how can you tell if an area is an opinion area? Good question, but not an easy one. When good brothers [and sisters...I asked Gordon if I could add "and sisters," while lovingly chiding him, "See what I mean?"] who love God and his word have consistent differences on a given subject, we had better guard ourselves from having dogmatic attitudes. To one, a given issue may seem quite clear, but the issue may be not at all clear to another. In such areas, abide by your own personal conscience, but avoid dogmatism.[2]

Easier said than done, right?

Hermeneutics

What's a hermeneutic, you ask? Our hermeneutic determines how we will interpret the scriptures. Our hermeneutic is the way in which we apply scripture, the way in which we ask, "How does this passage apply to my life today?" Hermeneutics is simply the study of the principles and methods of interpreting the texts of the Bible and determining what the text means to us today.[3]

We all have a hermeneutic—a way in which we apply scripture to our lives—but is our hermeneutic a good one? Until we understand a verse in its literary, historical, and cultural context we are not fully equipped to understand the verse's application for us today (if it has an application today). Again, our hermeneutic determines how we will interpret the scriptures. Is everything to be interpreted literally? If not, *when* not? For instance, how am I to take a scripture in the Old Testament that applied to Israel and apply it to my life today? How does culture define the scriptures, and what principles transcend culture? What is the context of what I am reading? What would the author's audience have understood? Is the scripture poetry, law, prophecy, or wisdom? How do we interpret metaphors, hyperboles, and figures of speech? So many misunderstandings of scripture come when we don't take these questions into account. These questions are at the heart of biblical interpretation.[4]

If we take a literal view of interpretation we could read just a few of Jesus' teachings and quickly end up sporting one hand and one eye (Matthew 5:29-30), hating our family (Luke 14:26), and carrying a wooden cross on our back (Luke 14:27). We know by compiling and learning Jesus' teachings that the attitudes of the heart are always his central focus. While Jesus makes the point in Matthew 5:29-30 that we need to take sin extremely seriously, we realize that cutting off our hand or gouging out our eye does not take away our desire to sin. We could take Jesus' words literally and cut off our right hand for stealing—wrongly thinking we are right with God because now we only steal with our left hand. We could gouge out an eye but continue to lust with the other eye (and with the mind's eye).

We may read instructions given to the early church and practices of early Christians—and wonder why we practice some and not others. For example: We don't often observe the Lord's Supper as a meal, as was the custom of the early Christians (1 Corinthians 11:20-22); instead, we practice a quick observance using grape juice and unleavened bread. Women don't wear veils to church, but often wear gold and pearls. Men don't raise their hands when they pray. Women may have braided hair or short hair, while men may be sporting long hair or "man buns" (1 Timothy 2:8-9). We don't often practice greeting each other with a holy kiss as Paul calls us to do (Romans 16:16; 1 Corinthians 16:20; 1 Thessalonian 5:26), and we don't abstain from eating the meat of animals that have been strangled, or from blood in our meat (Acts 15:20).

My friend Dan Demshar, a teacher trained in biblical languages, offered this helpful summary of five principles of Biblical interpretation:

1. We must understand what a scripture means in the context of the people to whom it was written.
2. We must understand some of the cultural differences going on within the text. We need to understand the differences and the similarities in the text as compared with our situation today. For example, when we read the account of David and Goliath, some similarities to our situation today could include:

   - a desire to defend God's name
   - trust in God in the midst of a formidable challenge
   - overcoming fear when faced with an ominous obstacle

   Differences in David's situation from ours would include:

   - An army is approaching to kill the children of God.
   - A giant is calling out a child of God (David) to face him in combat.
   - All people in this account live under Old Testament law, but we live under the New Testament covenants.
   - There is a physical nation of Israel that needs to defend itself against idolatrous nations.

   There can be differences in time, situation, culture, language, and the covenant (Old Testament covenant vs. New Testament covenant) when reading Scripture. We must be aware of these differences.

3. We must understand the theological principle in the text. Theological principles are ascertained from the text and are timeless principles that apply in both the Old Testament and New Testament covenant. These principles can be reflected in different cultures in different ways, but are not bound to any one culture.

   So, as we refer back to David and Goliath, examples of *possible* theological principles in the text that need to be tested could include:

- Trust in God when obstacles confront you.
- Kill your enemies with any means available when they oppose you.

Whoops. Something doesn't seem right about that last one, so we must compare the principle with other principles found in other places.

First, is the principle of trusting God when obstacles confront us consistent in both covenants? Do we see New Testament leaders trusting in God to overcome obstacles? Yes. Since we do, we can conclude that this is a theological principle applicable to different situations and covenants.

Second, does the principle of killing our enemies by any means available hold true across time, covenants, and cultures? Did the apostles slay those who opposed them as David killed Goliath? No. Since this is not true, we conclude that this is not a theological, timeless principle to be applied to situations in the New Testament. (Whew, that's a relief!)

4. We must check the principle we conclude against other principles found in other places to see if it is consistently applied.

We must determine whether other New Testament leaders trust in God in order to overcome obstacles. Since we do see them trusting in God to overcome obstacles we can conclude that this is a theological principle applicable to different situations and covenants.

We must also check to see if the apostles slayed those who opposed them, as David did Goliath. Since they did not, we conclude that this is not a theological, timeless principle to be applied to situations in the New Testament.

5. We make applications of the theological principles to different situations in our lives.

―⁓⁓―

The application of these five principles shows us that even though a principle is put in place in a particular time and culture for a specific situation, we may still find a theological principle that can be applied to other situations. That's what we look for. The principle may be timeless, or it may be instructional for a specific situation and time.

We must put all scriptures together, considering culture and context, in order to gain a more complete understanding of their meanings. Otherwise we may miss the point.

The Real Turning Point of Hermeneutics

Thus far, we have mentioned the importance of culture, literalism, and context in hermeneutics. We must consider such things carefully or we will fail to interpret biblical principles correctly. But what is the real turning point of hermeneutics when it comes to correctly understanding the role of women in the church today?

The most important element of hermeneutics is this: We must learn to accurately distinguish between instructions and principles that are merely cultural, and therefore temporary, and instructions and principles that are transcultural, and therefore permanent. This is the challenge that has dogged biblical interpreters (and we all interpret the Bible when we read it!) and resulted in many doctrinal differences and divisions throughout Christianity's two-thousand-year history.

This challenge is heightened when we are dealing with teachings that could be labeled "sensitive" or "controversial." Unfortunately, many people consider the woman's role to be among the most sensitive and controversial of subjects!

A helpful exercise is to take a different sensitive subject and consider how it might compare to our study of the woman's role. In this case, let us consider the difficult topic of slavery in the Bible. Slavery is an unsavory topic, but it can provide a valuable study tool in helping us to learn the difference between cultural, temporary teachings and transcultural, permanent principles. The topic of slavery provides an important precedent for modern biblical interpretation and application that can help us be consistent in the way we read, interpret, and apply the Bible. The time we spend digging more deeply into interpretative issues regarding slavery will prove worthwhile. Author and teacher Michael Burns shared the following thoughts on slavery with me. Please read carefully.

Let me be clear that I am in no way equating the plight of slaves with the role of women in the church. These are not comparable issues. What is helpful, though, is to consider briefly what the Bible says about slavery, how those passages have been interpreted and utilized in previous eras to justify slavery, and how modern Christians now interpret those same scriptures differently to *deny* slavery as an acceptable position for the Christian. Today you would be hard-pressed to find a Christian who would argue that the Bible condones slavery in the modern cultural context. Our goal in examining the topic of slavery is to analyze how people interpret scripture in cultural context. Once we see how we interpret the passages on slavery in a modern setting, it would make sense that we consistently apply that same method of interpretation to an issue like the role of women in the church. After all, any method of biblical interpretation and application that is inconsistent is problematic on many levels.

The Bible does not forbid any and all slavery, but rather regulates the practice among God's followers both in the Old Testament and New Testament. That fact is especially difficult to accept for those of us who understand the insidious way in which slavery was practiced in the United States for several centuries. Slavery was, with relatively few exceptions, applied in the harshest and most damaging ways imaginable. Unfortunately, during the seventeenth, eighteenth, and nineteenth centuries, the Bible was used to justify the institution, no matter how harshly slavery was practiced. (To read about the dramatic difference between slavery in the United States and slavery as it was often practiced in ancient Greco-Roman society, please see Appendix A.)

To avoid erroneous interpretations, we must understand that God has an *ideal* will and also an *allowed* will, the latter being designed to give way to the former as time and circumstances change. Prior to the Civil War, the American church was split on the issue of slavery in the Bible. Some argued that the Bible did not allow for the Christian to approve of such a blight against humanity. The majority, however, believed that slavery, and specifically, transatlantic slavery, was justifiable and defensible by proper biblical interpretation.

Defenders of slavery emphasized four clear points in the Bible:

multiple wives in O.T.
ideal? no

1. Christian masters were instructed about how to treat their slaves (Colossians 4:1; Ephesians 6:9).
2. Christian slaves were instructed about how to respect their masters (Ephesians 6:5–6; Colossians 3:22; 6:1–2; Titus 2:9).
3. Scripture dictates that slave and master have equal access to salvation, but no other manner of equality is expressly dictated (1 Corinthians 7:21–23; 12:13; Galatians 3:28; Colossians 3:11).
4. The Bible allowed slaveholders like Philemon to be church members. Because of this, most churches argued that without explicit condemnation of slavery and slaveholding in the Bible, as long as slavery was legal, the church could not declare slavery a sin. The church, and individual Christians could do nothing stronger than give lip service to denouncements of slavery based on personal dislike of the institution.

What the interpreters of the time seem to have overlooked were broader scriptural principles and the overall trajectory of God's will. They failed to consider the implications of Jesus as the full revelation of God's will (Hebrews 1:3), a will that had been only partially visible prior to Christ (Hebrews 1:1–2). They neglected the new paradigm that was created by Jesus' words, urging them to do unto others as they would have done to them (Matthew 7:12); they disregarded the call to imitate Christ in putting others' interests ahead of their own (Philippians 2:1–5).

They overlooked the trajectory of Paul's words, the target towards which he was aiming when he declared that there was no distinction in Christ between slave or free (Galatians 3:28; Colossians 3:11). They read past the true message of Paul's letter to Philemon, in which Paul urged the slaveholder Philemon to receive his slave Onesimus as a brother (Philemon 16) and even hinted that Philemon should free Onesimus if he fully understood what it meant to be in Christ (Philemon 21). The culturally-bound supporters of American slavery even managed to all but ignore the message of 1 Timothy 1:10, which lumped slave traders in with murderers, adulterers, liars, and other lawbreakers.

True, the Bible does contain verses that instruct both slaves and masters, and these verses might seem to implicitly endorse the whole concept of slavery if they are read at a simplistic, face-value level. And it is true that the Bible contains no verses that directly call for the end of slavery. However, when we take a big-picture look at the overarching message of the Bible, the ministry of Jesus, and the writings of Paul, we see that they clearly espouse a message of love and equality. As Paul shot the arrow of the gospel through the cultural fog of his day, he had to make some concessions to the world that was, even as he pointed people to the world God wanted. Sadly, the people who would later read his words and want to use them to justify slavery focused on the arrow itself, rather than the target it was speeding towards.

And what was that target? That target was a Christian community where love reigned. A community of equality and humility, with relationships based on unity in Christ and selfless love and putting the needs of others above self—as exemplified through the life and death of Jesus.[5]

Thus, it becomes clear that we cannot just read the Bible "literally" when we consider the topic of slavery. Paul was carefully addressing his cultural situation and leading the disciples *out of* their cultural biases, while at the same time being careful to avoid turning Christianity into a social movement. A change of one's heart, practices, and interactions within one's community will bring about social changes from the inside out.

Modern interpretations of the slavery passages in the New Testament have settled on four principles to direct our interpretation.

1. Slavery in the first century (the century in which Paul wrote) was dramatically different from the slavery we are familiar with in more recent history, so we must learn to read biblical passages considering those differences. (See Appendix A for a list detailing the differences between slavery as it was practiced in North America in the 1600s–1900s and slavery as it was practiced in biblical times.)

2. The New Testament never explicitly bans slavery and seems to tacitly condone it in places, but those passages must be understood in light of the larger principles of the gospel.

3. Paul was carefully but consistently moving the believing communities to principles governing the heart and attitude

rather than rules and regulations. Paul pointed Christians toward principles of mutual respect, humility, and a lack of favoritism.

4. Therefore, clear directives in favor of slavery in the New Testament are no longer applicable today if we read past the cultural conditions that Paul had to deal with and if we correctly apply the larger principles of the new covenant to our modern culture.[6]

If we were to consistently apply these same four general principles to the issue and topic of women's roles, how would that change the conversation? We can learn from the lessons in scriptural application and interpretation offered us by the slavery issue and strive for consistency as we examine women's role. Could it be possible that when considering the roles of women in the Christian community, we have at times overlooked the fact that Paul was carefully threading the needle of the cultural sensitivities of his day, while at the same time shooting the arrow of the gospel towards a larger target (Galatians 3:28; Colossians 3:11)? After all, Galatians 3:28 while describing equal access to salvation, not only says that in Christ there is neither slave nor free, but also that there is neither male nor female. Just how far does that equality go in both cases? Is it possible that we stress the "literal" and "clear" interpretation of passages such as 1 Corinthians 14:34 ("Women should remain silent in the churches") while overlooking other passages like 1 Corinthians 11:5 ("But every woman who prays or prophesies with her head uncovered dishonors her head")? The first scripture seems to forbid women to speak in church, while the second one assumes that women are prophesying and praying in church. Could we be guilty of staring at the arrow and neglecting the target? These are the kinds of questions that this book is addressing. Truth is the goal of all hermeneutics, even when those truths seem to be "hard" ones.[7]

Failure to consider cultural settings and God's trajectory toward an overarching target (relationships of unity and love) can cause angst in our faith journeys. We may read troublesome texts that record horrific acts blessed by God and legislation that was anything but perfect and wonder how this applies to building loving relationships.

The View from Paul's Window:

As theologian William J. Webb explains,

> We ultimately must come to grips with certain "repugnant moments" in the museum of patriarchy and "unpleasant pictures" in the halls of slavery. Without placing certain components within these texts into a culture-component classification, many of us would struggle in our Judeo-Christian faith....Only a redemptive-movement hermeneutic [one that looks at the trajectory toward the target of God's perfect plan made available through the death and resurrection of Jesus] adequately deals with these texts.... The Christian who embraces a redemptive-spirit approach cannot help but be profoundly influenced by the resilient character of the ancient text as it continues to speak to our modern world.[8]

Paul takes his cues from Jesus' life and teachings, where love and grace are paramount. When Jesus calls us to honor one another above ourselves and to love our neighbor as ourselves, he addresses our heart and seeks to transform it. A heart that embraces Jesus' loving, selfless attitude simply will not tolerate slavery and will not treat women with lesser value or honor. Jesus knows that over time, culture does change—but it only changes after many individuals have changed their hearts (Matthew 5:1–16). Jesus learned to function within his culture (a culture quite different from his familiar heavenly culture). He lived and sought to bring change word by word, individual by individual, day by day. He worked through a spiritual revolution, not a political or cultural revolution.

Background and Culture Matter: The Garden's Culture and Redemption's Counterculture

Imagine that you work in a large and diverse company and travel to various countries. First stops: West Africa, the Middle East, and Russia. When you arrive in each country, your work associates all ask you how you are. You give them a thumbs-up, then wonder why they react with shock and horror. (In those nations, giving someone a thumbs-up is the American equivalent of giving them the middle finger.)

You then travel to Turkey and greet a colleague. You have one hand in your pocket when you say hello, and your Turkish friend immediately perceives you as proud. (In Turkey, greeting someone with a hand in your pocket is considered arrogant.) You notice lush green grass, take off your shoes, and lay down and put your feet up. In so doing, you offend your Arab, Muslim, Hindu, and Buddhist colleagues by the disrespectful act of showing the soles of your feet.

Next stop: Japan. As you walk through your hotel, feeling comfortable in your "casual Friday" flip-flops and sweatpants, your Japanese colleagues wonder why you are so disrespectful. (In Japan, wearing sweatpants and flip-flops in public is considered disrespectful.)

Within one business trip, you have managed to disrespect and alienate the majority of your colleagues—not a great trip! What's the point? We can appear disrespectful, arrogant, and lewd to someone in another culture without even realizing it.

We know that world cultures are extremely diverse, but often we are so comfortable in and familiar with our own culture that we don't see clearly beyond its boundaries—in fact, it doesn't always occur to us that there *are* boundaries to our own culture. We forget that others may not see life the same way we do. Our perspective on what is proper, modest, kind, and respectful varies greatly depending on the culture that exists outside of "our window."

I am a United States citizen. I was born in the Southern United States but have lived half of my life in New England. I am white and from the middle class, which I realize brings me certain privileges I have not earned. My youngest son spent his first twelve years living in an orphanage in the developing world. Because we have such different life experiences, my beloved son and I—who now have shared many years of life together—have remarkably different perspectives on some things.

Even within my own country, culture varies greatly between regions. My daughter was once strongly chastised by my father-in-law when she asked him, "How are *you guys* doing?" My father-in-law considered her use of "you guys" to be inappropriate and disrespectful. My daughter genuinely wanted to know how her grandparents were doing, but quickly learned that *you guys* was not a term appreciated by Southern gentlemen like her grandfather; however, *y'all* would have been acceptable. Where I live (in the suburbs of Boston), people don't even know what *y'all* means! In the South, calling someone "Sweetie" or "Honey" is sort of like saying hello, but in Massachusetts, such endearments are considered condescending at best and akin to sexual harassment at worst. Where I live, people say, "Wicked awesome!" to describe something wonderful (here the word *wicked* can mean "extremely"). But many of the Southerners I grew up with would be thoroughly confused by this phrase, because in the South, *wicked* means "vile" and "corrupt."

And these are just language differences in my own country; when we travel abroad the differences multiply—not just with language, but also with our perspective on gender roles. The treatment and regard for women varies greatly from culture to culture and nation to nation. The church is not exempt from the influence of culture, although the church by very definition must strive to be countercultural.

As a young girl, I noticed that the women in my church were sweet and kind, but were relegated to "womanly roles" such as teaching children, cooking food, and laundering baptismal garments. I don't mean to discount or undervalue such contributions—all are meaningful acts of service in God's church—but as a child I often wished I had been born a male so I could do more to "change the world." Thankfully, I was inspired by an older woman who taught the Bible to her neighbors and to other women in the church. Her example greatly encouraged my eager young soul. She mentored me and prayed with me every week from the time I was fourteen years old until I got married. I began to imagine that perhaps a woman could play a significant role in the kingdom of God.

When my husband went into the ministry after college, he earned a master's degree in Bible in Abilene, Texas. I had just graduated from college and was leading some campus women's Bible discussions, but at that time in my church, with very few exceptions, only the men went into the ministry as a full-time (paid) job. While Wyndham and I lived in Texas, I wanted to take classes and perhaps get my graduate degree, but according to my husband, my job (and please no haters here, this was simply the culture of the time—he has since changed his views, profusely apologized, and encourages me in my current graduate studies) was simply to type his handwritten papers. (As an aside, with no application whatsoever to this subject, I think every person under the age of forty should experience the "joy" of typing long papers using carbon paper and Wite-Out, with a dictionary for spelling reference at your side.)

It was a man's world, both in the world and in the church. (Numerous Christian schools did not allow women to take part in their Bible graduate studies. When Wyndham was in graduate school, a woman could not major in Bible at his school.)[9]

The things I experienced in church growing up were simply part of my church culture. At that time it would have been considered "out of line" (and unbiblical) for women to participate in the congregational worship through "part-leading" (singing the alto or soprano part on stage for all to hear), sharing their thoughts or testimonies, praying publicly, ushering, or baptizing—and yet women in our fellowship now do all of these things. The woman's role has changed dramatically in a relatively short time in my own church, and yet many of my young millennial friends can't remember church any other way and still feel that the church limits women's roles too much. The discussion of women's roles affects us in various ways.

I was touched by a friend (a father and a leader in the church) who responded to me after reviewing a copy of an earlier manuscript of this book. He is a father of daughters, and he shared,

> Your book stirred up many emotions for me. First, it brought to the forefront my personal reflection on how being a dad of daughters and no sons affects my role in God's kingdom. I've at times lamented the lesser influence I may have because the people I can most influence in this world are female. Some Old Testament narratives and earthly culture suggest the notion I have failed in some way by not having a son. It's hard for me to separate from that notion, and I've felt that certain scriptures and the way I've understood them only perpetuate it. I cry as I type this, tapping into this feeling that, frankly, I have suppressed unknowingly. If I feel less valuable because of this notion, I can only imagine how my daughters (wife, mother, sisters, etc.) feel. The transcending gospel message rejects this notion, and I need to take that thought captive and make it obedient to Christ.

My prayer in writing this book is to guide us in exploring the heart of God as he speaks through Paul's writings on the role of women in the church. Do we as a church have further to go in learning to view and value women as Jesus intended, or have we gone too far? I believe these questions have answers, but the answers will be clearer if we first travel back through time and explore other cultures in order to gain greater perspective.

The Garden Culture

For practical purposes, let's start at the beginning. What was God's intent as he created women? From there, let us examine the progression and digression of women's value through different times and cultures.

In the creation account, many scholars believe that Genesis 2 describes the beautiful intent of God as he created man and woman: Man and woman fully complemented each other, walked without shame or adversity, and were responsible for the care of all created beings. Then comes Genesis 3, when sin enters the world through the first couple. These scholars believe that the consequences for Adam and Eve, such as the words spoken to Eve in Genesis 3:16, "I will greatly increase your pains in childbearing; with pain you will give birth to children. Your desire will be for your husband, and he will rule over you," are simply descriptions of the way life would be after sin entered the world—in other words, inequality between genders was part of the result of sin and not the way God originally intended life to be. New Testament scholar Scot McKnight explains this saying:

descriptive not prescriptive

> Sadly, some think Genesis 3:16 is a *prescription* for the relationships of women and men for all time. Instead of *prescription,* the two lines are a *prediction* of the fallen desire of fallen women and fallen men in a fallen condition in a fallen world.
>
> Fallen women yearn to dominate the man, and fallen men yearn to dominate women. The desire to dominate is a broken desire. The redeemed desire is to love in mutuality. This verse in Genesis 3, in other words, predicts a struggle of fallen wills; they don't prescribe how we are *supposed* to live.[10]

This interpretation, which is compelling to me, views the Fall as the time when tension and power struggle first began between genders. With the onset of disobedience to God, dysfunction entered the first family in the form of blame, shame, and competition. This unfortunate heritage was passed down to Adam and Eve's children, with comparison and ego leading one son to murder another.

Jesus' redemption offers us the chance to get family and gender roles right, to function as we were intended before sin entered the world. In his days on earth Jesus reached out to, accepted, respected, and honored not only women, but also children, Gentiles, lepers, and outcasts of all sorts. His understanding of equality was far broader than that of most humans—both in his own time and in ours.

In this life, we as individuals and the church as a collective body are always undergoing the sanctification process. Only in heaven will we be fully perfected. Meanwhile, we are works in progress both individually and collectively. Being works in progress means we should not stay the same but should continually make progress in our own walk with God, in our relationships with one another, and in our understanding of God's word.

Helpmeet or Image Bearer?

The words used in the creation of woman speak volumes about

the value and purpose for which women were created.

Genesis 2:18 describes the newly created woman as man's helper. The Hebrew word translated "helper" is *ezer* (*ezer* rhymes with *razor*). So what's an *ezer*? In Genesis 2:18 this word has often been translated "helpmeet," which indicates that woman is subservient to man; I (and many others) dispute this translation as inaccurate. Let's take a closer look at this word. *Ezer* appears 21 times in the Old Testament, with a variety of meanings:

- 2 times in Genesis the word is referred to as "woman"
- 3 times it refers to nations to whom Israel appealed for military aid
- 16 times it refers to God as being Israel's helper (see Deuteronomy 33:26, 29; Psalm 33:20; and Hebrews 13:6)

What then can be said about the relationship between the helper and the person being helped? In every instance where the word is used, the person being helped is presented as the primary person whose interests are at stake—the one *being helped* is the one in need.

In Genesis 2:18 and 20 the person whose primary interests are at stake is Adam. He is the primary person tasked with working and taking care of the Garden, and he is the one in need. The woman (Eve) is the person who will render assistance to Adam to help him meet that goal. There is no indication of superiority or inferiority. Eve is simply using her gifts to supply aid. The kind of help the man needs demands full use of the woman's strengths and gifts.

Conceivably, "taking a rib" from Adam means that God took a good portion of Adam's side, since the man considers the woman to be "bone of his bone" and "flesh of his flesh." This picture describes the intimacy between man and woman as they stand as equals before God.[11]

In her compelling book, *Half the Church*, Carolyn Custis James elaborates on the meaning of ezer:

> God calls the first woman *ezer*—a name that is used most frequently in the Old Testament for God himself. In a profound sense, God named his firstborn daughter after himself. God is Israel's *ezer*. For God's female image bearers, *ezer* defines a way in which women are uniquely called to reflect

God. "Like Father like daughter," as the saying goes. Our Father is an *ezer*, and we are *ezers* too.[12]

The full Hebrew word for the woman as the suitable helper is *ezer kenegdo*. *Ezer* is translated "helper." *Kenegdo* is translated "suitable to him"—in older English, it was translated "meet." The old word *helpmeet* (used in the King James Version, translated in 1611) has led to interpretations that view woman's God-given role as the man's assistant and wife, as the mother of his children and manager of his home. If this is the true meaning of the translation, it means that women who are not wives or mothers are not fulfilling their God-given roles. It leaves out approximately sixty percent of the females (in the United States) who are neither wives nor mothers. This can make women who are not married feel like second-class citizens at home and in the church.[13]

Phil Lasarsky, a teacher from the Midwest family of churches, wrote to me,

> Ez'er kenegdo, used in Genesis 2:18, is most often rendered in English translations as "helper" or "assistant," with the implication that the helper or assistant is an inferior. Throughout the Tanakh (that is, the Hebrew Bible), ez'er usually does not indicate anything about status or subordination, nor does it describe a person's role. Rather, the word indicates the action of helping, supporting, or providing the means that enables another to be successful in attaining a goal. Most of the time the *ez'er* role is Adonai "assisting" Isra'el.[14]

The meaning of *kenegdo* indicates that woman is man's match—literally, she is someone in front of him, corresponding to him, neither inferior nor superior, but equal.

Oneness is the predominant theme in translating *ezer kenegdo*. Experiencing oneness with someone doesn't erase individuality; rather, each person benefits and is enriched by the differences. When the two are combined, the two of them align with God. Genesis 2:24 would have shocked the original readers of Genesis: "That is why a man leaves his father and mother and is united to his wife, and they become one flesh." This description of men clinging to their wives is backward from the patriarchal world of old, in which the wife leaves her parents and is absorbed into her husband's family.[15]

God has showcased numerous women *ezers*, perhaps so we can greater understand their strength and valor. The Old Testament is full of heroines of faith, flawed but still faithful: Sarah, the mother of Israel; Miriam, the prophetess who led Isreal with Moses and Aaron (Micah 6:4); Abigail, who persuaded a king; Deborah, a judge and prophetess; Esther, the queen who saved God's people; Rahab, a harlot who saved the spies and was in the lineage of Jesus; and Jael, who killed Sisera with a tent peg. All these women portray the strength of faith filled-women, or *ezers*.

I think of these women as God's "Wonder Women" of old. While we might picture a woman like Esther living a royal and pampered life as a queen, this was not actually the case. Kings had harems. Competition for the king's attention was brutal. Women like Esther were strong, flawed, but faithful women whose stories God gives us to inspire us.

In the years between the Old and New Testament, the value of women began deteriorating. Historical records, such as the Apocrypha, include writings from Ben Sirach, who wrote *Ecclesiasticus*, a compilation of ethical teachings from approximately 200–175 BC, the largest wisdom book preserved from antiquity. His writings included such teachings:

- Good wives and mothers are to be respected, but if you don't like your wife or mother, you should not trust her; keep careful records of supplies you issue to a woman. (Sir 2:6–7)
- Deed no property to a woman. (3:20; 25:22–26)
- Don't let a woman support you. (33:20; 25:2–26)
- Women are responsible for sin coming into the world and their spite is unbearable. (25:13–26)
- Daughters are a disaster, a total loss, and a constant potential source of shame (Sir 7:242–9; 22:3–5; 26:9–12; 42:9–11)

And these were just a few of the writings about women during this time.[16]

By the first century, women were not highly valued in many cultures, as we will explore in the following chapter. It's hard for me to imagine living in that culture. Jesus arrived on earth and conducted his ministry in this environment.

Thankfully, Jesus had a different plan. A restoration of unity—life as it should be, relationships as God intended.

Jesus and Women

Jesus' ministry displayed a distinctly radical departure from the gender inequality so prevalent in the ancient Middle East. As we have seen, Jewish women in Jesus' day were considered inferior to men. But Jesus was a radical barrier-breaker in the value he gave to women. In a distinctly counter-cultural practice, Jesus had women traveling with him in his band of disciples. Some women even funded his travels (Luke 8:1–3).

Kenneth Bailey, in his informative and inspiring book, *Jesus Through Middle Eastern Eyes,* notes that Jesus deliberately shaped his teachings in order to powerfully communicate his message both to men and women. He purposely used examples of both men and women in his examples and parables. In Luke 4:25–27, Naaman the Syrian wasn't the only unlikely hero—Jesus also praised the widow of Zarephath! Other instances of profiling both men and women in his teaching include:

- Twin parables of the mending of a garment (a task typically performed by a woman) and the making of wine (the task of a man) (Luke 5:36–39).

- Jesus' protective love for repentant sinners of both genders: the sinful woman (Luke 7:36–50) and the male tax collector with the Pharisee (Luke 18:9–14).

- Two prayers offering assurance that prayers will be answered, exemplified in stories about a man and a woman (Luke 11:5–15 is about a man and Luke 18:1–8 is about a woman).

- The parable of a man planting a mustard seed is linked to the story of a woman kneading leaven into dough (Luke 13:18–21).[17]

When Jesus spoke with the Samaritan woman at the well, he crossed all kinds of barriers: racial, cultural, intellectual, gender, and class. He showed us that women have the same mission as men (see John 4:4–26).

Jesus' relationship with Mary and Martha also broke the cultural rules of the day. In Acts, Paul describes himself as sitting at the feet of Gamaliel (Acts 22:3). To sit at the feet of a rabbi often meant one was a disciple of the rabbi. Mary did not just "beg out of helping Martha in the kitchen," but became a disciple of Rabbi Jesus as she sat at his feet. Martha, as we know from the story, is distracted from the teachings of Jesus by her cooking and preparations.

In the Middle Eastern cultural context, Martha is naturally understood to be upset because her younger sister is seated with the men and has become a disciple of Rabbi Jesus instead of helping in the kitchen. Martha is perhaps less concerned about needing help in the kitchen than she is worried about what people will think about Mary's bold (even presumptuous) move. This was a big deal. Would Mary even be allowed to marry after sitting alongside the men at a rabbi's feet? What would the neighbors say? Jesus defended Mary's right to become his disciple and to continue her "theological studies."[18] The traditional cultural separation between men and women no longer applied when Jesus was present. He changed everything.

As the cross approached, the women in Jesus' band of disciples became more prominent as they joined the Twelve to support Jesus' ministry. Women were last at the cross (Matthew 27:55–56) and first to be given the message of the resurrection (Matthew 28:8–10). Jesus actually rebuked the Eleven for not listening to the women who reported that Jesus was no longer in the tomb (Mark 16:14). After the resurrection, women heard the same teaching and joined in the same fellowship. They attended the first recorded prayer meeting (Acts 1:14), were the first to greet Christian missionaries (Acts 16:13), and a woman was the first European convert (Acts 16:14).

Jesus' view and treatment of men and women came from the heart of God. God is not concerned with outward appearance, but with the attitudes of our hearts.

> "The LORD does not look at the things people look at. People look at the outward appearance, but the LORD looks at the heart." (1 Samuel 16:7)

Paul's Window Seat

It's fair to say that you and I can't know what it was like to live in the Middle East two thousand years ago. The only one who can truly know what a culture is like is one who is part of that culture.

Paul's window seat—whether in a prison cell, a synagogue, or a Greek temple— allowed him to view life from his particular vantage point. Though we can assemble only a fragmented picture of the culture of Paul's day through historical letters, archaeological findings, and historical documents, we can be sure Paul's culture was significantly different than the one in which we live.

To better understand Paul's teachings, we must look at the cultures to which (and in which) he was writing. When the first-century cultural picture is removed, the window from which we view Paul's instructions is tainted by our current and modern views, whether we realize it or not. We read his words through our own experiences, understandings, and cultural habits—just as I once saw that "evil" beer in my friend's fridge.

Let's begin exploring Paul's window view by asking an important big-picture question: What might life have been like for a woman during the time of Jesus and Paul?

Jesus was born and lived during the early days of the Roman Empire (27 BC–1453 AD), and the early church was established during the Roman Empire. It is important that we understand the predominant cultures of the time, as the Roman Empire was spreading through all the existing cultures. Many cultures influenced the environment in which New Testament women lived, including Greek, Macedonian, Jewish, Cretan, and Roman.

Greco-Roman society placed women in a lesser role than they had enjoyed in the past. From the Laws of the Twelve Tables (a Roman law code, circa 450 BC—twelve tablets with laws written on them), we learn that women were the protected property of the leading male into whose household they were born.[19] In Greco/Roman society, most women were not educated.

Let's look more closely at the way women were treated in some of the different cultures that coexisted during the Roman era.

Greek Women

If you were a woman in the Greek culture, your public appearances would be limited and your sphere of influence would be your home. Greek women lived in separate women's quarters. No one came to these quarters except their husbands. They didn't appear at meals, never walked the street alone, and never went to public assemblies.

The noted exceptions were women who "worked" outside of the home—and their work was akin to upper-class prostitution. The Greeks had a well-organized and profitable business for women—these women, called *hetaerae*, were similar to Japanese geisha girls. The *hetaerae* provided men with entertainment, conversation, and sexual favors at dinner parties (or after-parties). The few Athenian women who were educated and who could discuss current literature and philosophical thought were, for the most part, among these courtesans, the *hetaerae*.

The Greek temple of Aphrodite (located northwest of the Ancient Agora in Athens) had a thousand priestesses who were temple prostitutes, so it's easy to see that sensuality and immorality were large parts of this culture.

Respectable women didn't attend public assemblies. If a Christian woman who lived in a Greek town had taken an active part or a speaking role in the church's work, the church would have inevitably gained the reputation of being a gathering place for loose women.[20]

We see Paul's sensitivity to the Greek culture in his instructions to women:

> So I counsel younger widows to marry, to have children, to manage their homes and to give the enemy no opportunity for slander. (1 Timothy 5:14)

> Likewise, teach the older women to be reverent in the way they live,

not to be slanderers or addicted to much wine, but to teach what is good. Then they can urge the younger women to love their husbands and children, to be self-controlled and pure, to be busy at home, to be kind, and to be subject to their husbands, so that no one will malign the word of God. (Titus 2:3–5)

Macedonian Women

Women of Macedonia had greater independence and importance in public affairs than their Greek counterparts. Macedonian women were greatly influenced by the "rich and famous," including the country's princesses (Macedonia had a monarchy). Women often imitated the style and values of these celebrities.

Jewish Women

Jewish women had little value in their culture as it moved away from teachings in the Old Testament. In Jewish law a woman was not a person but a thing. Women, slaves, and children were classed together. They were not qualified to testify in court as witnesses and were the property of their husbands. Their education was limited, as they generally married and began having children at a young age. In the synagogue, they did not share in worship, but were segregated from the men in a separate galley or other part of the building. They were exempt from fulfilling religious duties that had to be performed at specific times, as their first duties were to home and children. Women were forbidden to teach in a school, even to young children.

A Jewish woman would never talk to a man in public, not even to her husband.

A Jewish prayer book even contained this prayer for men: "Blessed art thou, O Lord our God, who has not made me a woman."[21]

A Jewish woman's purity and modesty were of great importance. The Talmud, a book of Jewish tradition collected a little later, around 400–500 AD, records a discussion of what womanly features might arouse sexual excitement in a male: a woman's leg (referencing Isaiah 47:2), a woman's voice (referencing Song of Songs 2:14), a woman's hair (referencing Song of Songs 4:1).

A "rule" from the Talmud stated, "A bad man who sees his wife go out with her hair unfastened and spin cloth in the street with her armpits uncovered and bathe with the men...such a one it is a religious duty to divorce."²² In other words, a woman who wore her hair unfastened was equally as offensive as one who bathed with a man. Jesus showcased a radical perspective when he praised the sinful woman who had dried his feet with her hair, as a woman was only supposed to let her hair down in the presence of her husband (see Luke 7:36–50).

A Rabbinic "exposition" of Genesis 2:21–22 states,

> God did not form woman out of the head, lest she become proud; nor out of the eye, lest she should lust; nor out of the ear, lest she should be curious; nor out of the mouth, lest she be talkative; nor out of the heart, lest she be jealous; nor out of the hand, lest she should be covetous; nor out of the foot, lest she should be a wandering busybody; but out of a rib, which was always covered; therefore modesty should be her primary quality.²³

Cretan Women

Crete was a Greek island to which Paul sent his letter to Titus. Cretan women lived in quite a different culture from the Jews. Cretan views of women were ahead of their time in terms of respect, protection, legal rights, and financial independence.

Sexual offenses carried penalties for the male offender even if the woman was a slave. Citizens of Crete referenced their country as the motherland (whereas other countries used the masculine "fatherland"), and deities were often feminine. Beginning in 450 BC, Cretan women had more legal rights relating to inheritance. When a Cretan woman was divorced or widowed, she would legally keep her property and half of whatever she had woven.

Roman Women

The Roman Empire (27 BC–1453 AD) grew quickly, and Roman culture had penetrated many other cultures in Asia, Europe, and the Middle East by the time Jesus arrived on earth. Women were gradually given more freedom, higher legal status, and a greater power and influence. Women frequently held civil offices, served as priestesses, and served not only in traditional roles as wives, mothers, and midwives, but also as physicians, musicians, artists, athletes, manufacturers, and commercial entrepreneurs.²⁴ Prostitutes were also present in Roman society.

Such was the setting in which Paul wrote. While Paul has often been accused of teaching sexual inequality, I believe he actually opposed the demeaning treatment of women that was so prevalent in his cultural setting. But many of the people who first quoted Paul had been influenced by centuries of Greek philosophy. They saw through the window of their own culture and customs—in a sense, they read Paul's words through the eyes of Aristotle (who had created many laws and teachings suppressing and devaluing women).[25] When Greek philosophy began to infuse Christian theology—as Paul's words began to be interpreted through the viewpoints of Aristotle and of Stoic philosophers—Paul's message (that women should learn and husbands are to lay down their lives for their wives) was often lost and his words were used to promote positions he had actually opposed.

The New Woman: The Burning of the ~~Bras~~ (Veils)

Those of us who are "baby boomers" remember the 1960s, when culture made a dramatic and deviant turn. In a short time, we went from conservative television shows like *Father Knows Best* and *Leave It to Beaver* to a world in which sex, drugs, and rock and roll dominated the scene. A new culture began to emerge, perhaps in reaction to abuses and problems younger people perceived in the culture they'd been handed by the generations before.

This movement pressed for equal rights for women in the workplace, for language that was inclusive for women rather than male-centric, for a woman's ability to make decisions about her own body, for access to all programs of education (including sports), for the sharing of household roles, and for greater inclusion in the political process.

History repeats itself again and again (from Adam's rib to women's lib), and pendulums swing back and forth in reaction. In a similar but perhaps even more influential way, two thousand years earlier a huge culture change had emerged in the mid-40s AD (as in, the year 40 AD) with the arrival of the "new wives" or "new women." We find repeated references to this shift from multiple sources writing in the late Republic and the early second century AD, including the writings of poets and playwrights and legislation by the Emperor Augustus seeking to limit this new phenomenon.[26]

In the beginning of the first century the increased wealth flowing into Rome and the political instability from civil wars combined to create an unstable social setting in which women from elite families gained political influence. Social norms were fragile during the first century in Rome, resulting in tested and/or broken traditional boundaries. Families were shrinking, and some people thought this was in part due to women's lack of interest in motherhood. We can't know for sure the extent of the influence of the "new women." Was the worldliness and sensuality limited to Roman elite women, or were the "new women" imagined to some extent? Were these women profiled, and their influence exaggerated, in order to create political smears? We don't know that, but we do know that their existence was recorded by various poets and writers in Paul's day.[27]

The "new wife" or "new woman" of Roman culture was thought to pursue her own pleasure, social life, and extramarital liaisons, often at the expense of her own family and household—this was a women's lib movement way before our time.[28] The shift may have been a reaction to the discrimination women had experienced during the intertestamental period and a rebellion against the traditional roles and rules held by the previous generation. (For a brief historical overview of women's history from the second century through the Restoration Movement, see Appendix B. In the Restoration period alone, some women served as missionaries and preachers, yet a few years later, women were said to be in danger of hell for standing at a podium or wearing pants.)

As the women of the 1960s brought change in their day, so the women of the AD 40s–60s brought change in theirs. What were some of the changes? Property was no longer automatically transferred to a woman's husband upon marriage. This meant that the new woman had the financial freedom to dissolve her marriage and get back some or all of her dowry. The new woman might not want to spoil her figure with pregnancy and might endanger her life with dangerous contraception and abortions. If a new woman got pregnant, she might despise the thought of nursing her own child; instead, she would employ a wet nurse. The female figure was esteemed, and so the new woman dressed extravagantly with gold, pearls, expensive attire, and extravagant hairstyles.

Then as now, media shaped culture. The theater was a prominent institution of Roman culture. Older women with wealth and sensual prowess (the mature embodiment of the new woman) became established characters in Roman comedy and theater. These characters reinforced and influenced society and morals with their propaganda. Younger women often took on the values espoused by the older, more "cultured" women, and women's values and behavior in relationships followed suit.

The new churches to which Paul was writing were still in their infancy and were being affected by Roman influence as culture changed during the 50s and 60s (that is, 50–60 AD). Remember that Paul wrote the Corinthian letters between 53 and 57 AD, and he composed his two letters to Timothy between 62 and 67 AD. (According to 1 Corinthians 5:9, and suggested by 2 Corinthians, Paul had written previous letters to the Corinthians. We do not have these letters.)

Painting the Picture

New wives, new women, male backlash: It is possible that this is the cultural environment in which Paul was writing. Facts and descriptions don't always paint a clear enough picture of history. If we could travel back in time to visit a typical first-century worship service in Corinth, we might have met some women like these imaginary characters—women from different backgrounds who all had moved to Corinth for different reasons. I am deliberately highlighting the differences between the women in this made-up scenario:

Anna had been raised in a typical Greek family in Galatia. She heard the message of Jesus through a family member, and she and her husband became Christians. The women in Anna's Galatian church, like most Greek women, stayed at home, had separate quarters, and did not attend public assemblies. Once Anna became a Christian, she began worshipping with the church, but was still treated as a second-class citizen, especially by the Judaizers. Paul sent a letter to Anna's church, appealing to the Jewish Christians who were trying to preach salvation through law rather than through faith. Anna marveled as Paul's letter was read in the assembly:

> "For you are all children of God through faith in Christ Jesus. And all who have been united with Christ in baptism have put on the character of Christ, like putting on new clothes. There is no longer Jew or Gentile, slave or free, male and female. For you are all one in Christ Jesus. And now that you belong to Christ, you are the true children of Abraham. You are his heirs, and God's promise to Abraham belongs to you."

What an incredible new teaching! The church slowly began accepting the women, but it took time. Anna's husband was slow to accept her as a person with equal value, but even so, Anna felt new hope and anticipation for the future. Several years later, Anna and her family moved to Corinth.

Dafina, from Macedonia, enjoyed much more freedom as a woman than Anna did. A dealer of cloth, Dafina had been converted by a business associate named Lydia. Dafina's husband's business took him to Corinth, and so Dafina transferred and resumed her business there.

Rachel came from a long lineage of Jews. Her grandfather was a Pharisee. Rachel and her mother were baptized after her cousin's family shared the good news of Jesus with them. Rachel's Jewish father divorced her mom because of her new faith. Rachel and her mother moved to a region in Corinth when Jewish friends and family members, also converts to Christ, invited them in.

Ariana, a widow, was from Crete and supported herself with weaving. She moved to Corinth because a friend wanted Ariana to meet her brother, an eligible single Christian man.

Julia, from Rome, was a sophisticated woman and a civil leader when she came to Christ. She had moved to Corinth to help care for her husband's aging parents.

Cecelia, known by her friends as "Lady Gogo," had worked as a high-end prostitute before she became a Christian. She had changed her life, but had been entrenched in the culture of the new woman for several years. She had been born and raised in Corinth and found it awkward at times to meet new brothers who she had earlier "visited" at after-parties.

Porcia, an only child from Rome, was a divorced woman. Having been left a large inheritance, she was into high fashion and all the trimmings available to the new woman. She wore exquisite, expensive, and fashionable clothes and "wicked high hair" (as they say in New England). Her jewelry came from the most expensive shop in town. She had season tickets to the Roman theatre.

These women came into contact with each other through the Corinthian church. Since her recent arrival, Anna had become enamored by Porcia's sophistication and Lady Gogo's boldness. Julia and Porcia had taken Anna to the theater with them, and she had been enthralled with the glamour of the new woman. Porcia wore the latest fashion and men turned their heads when she walked by. This enticed Anna to want to be more like her—in a sort of 1960s "bra-burning" move, she threw out her *stola* (head covering), and Ariana followed suit. Ariana had long felt that women needed to stand up for their rights. As a widow, she had learned to take care of her own needs through her weaving business. Her gesture (removing her head covering) signified her independence. Julia had also started to imitate Porcia's high fashion.

One Sunday in March in the mid-50s, the church came together to worship in Corinth as usual. This particular Sunday was the first time all of these women were together at the same time for the public assembly.

As Lady Gogo and Porcia entered the assembly, they stood out because they did not wear the customary head covering signifying modesty, respect, and morality.

To say that Rachel was shocked that day—the first time she had worshiped with the Corinthian church—would be an understatement. First of all, communion seemed to her to be equated with party time. People were actually getting drunk! It was loud and crazy. Julia, Lady Gogo, and Porcia had a "lively" communion. As the church members were prophesying and speaking in tongues, Lady Gogo, Porcia and Julia, emboldened from the communion wine, became disruptive. Even Dafina, who at first had kept quiet, joined in. Having been on her own for a while, Anastasia now felt free to question the authority of the men leading the service; she leaned over to her new acquaintance, Rachel, to whisper criticisms. Anna, who had never been adequately instructed since teaching was not available for woman in her cultural background, finally felt liberated and made her joy known with her wild screams of, *"Eleútheraí esmén!"* ("We are free!"). Rachel pulled her veil tightly over her face and fainted.

This imaginary cultural-clashing scene is hard to imagine from my window, where orderly ushers (and usherettes) pass communion trays of grape juice and I take my tiny cup and remember Jesus. I already know the order of service, as I received it via email the day before.

How different my modern church experience is from worship

in Corinth at a time when things had gotten out of hand. In Galatia, the fictional Anna had taken hope from Paul's earlier letter, which had given her confidence as he taught salvation for all through faith in Christ. But there in Corinth, were we to continue this scene, Anna would have heard the same Paul urgently exclaim the ancient equivalent of, "Put a sock in it! Get yourselves in order, get a grip, shut up, and straighten up! Who could ever come in here and see the heart and life of Jesus?" While this story is fictitious, my goal is to paint a picture showing just how different "church" was in Corinth from what we experience today.

No wonder it can be difficult to grasp Paul's message in his letters to early churches! On the one hand he had to address Jewish Christians who were suppressing women; on the other hand perhaps he had to rein in the "new women" who were so excited about their newfound freedoms that they were taking their freedom to ungodly excesses. And people from both cultural extremes were moving to cities like Corinth and trying to worship together in a single fellowship—what a potential for mess and conflict! Whether the historical scene actually looked something like this fictitious scene, or whether the disorder resulted from women talking amongst themselves, throwing out questions, and causing various disruptions—whatever the source and appearance of the problem, Paul had to deal with disorder in the church so the young church could shine as a light to the world.

Paul had to counsel both ends of the cultural spectrum while also ministering to a wide range of perspectives in the middle, with the end goal of unity and godliness—God's culture.

These dilemmas help us understand why Paul had to make *allowances* in some of his letters to specific congregations. He had to address them *where they were in the moment,* while still moving them toward a more godly view of gender relations.

Paul's Teachings: A Broad-Strokes Overview

In his letter to Galatia, Paul writes boldly of freedom in Christ, arguing against restrictions and legalism, against following the Jewish law as opposed to embracing the grace and new covenant given by Christ. "It is for freedom that Christ has set us free!" he writes. "Stand firm, then, and do not let yourselves be burdened again by a yoke of slavery" (Galatians 5:1). In the same letter, Paul teaches that we are all equal (Galatians 3:28), which might lead a reader to conclude that Paul was opposed to slavery.

But in his letters to Timothy, Titus, and the Corinthian church, Paul lists a number of criticisms and rules limiting the behavior of women and instructing slave-owners in how to treat their slaves. He lays out rules for slaves and masters (Ephesians 6:5-9; Colossians 3:22, 4:1; Titus 2:9), and for women and men (1 Corinthians 14:26-35; 1 Timothy 2:8-14; Ephesians 5:22-29). At first glance, in these letters it seems that Paul is focused on restriction, not freedom.

So, which does Paul believe? The message of freedom from the law he writes to the Galatians, or the seeming message of "rules" and the acceptance of inequality he sends to Timothy, Titus, and the Corinthians?

Perhaps the timeless principle tells us that a Christlike attitude is expected in all relationships that have a sense of order to them—a sense that one person is in a position of responsibility, leadership, or authority, and that the other is in a position of following and even submission. Let's consider the example of a business owner and an employee (both of whom are Christians; gender is not at issue in this example). Both Christians are free and equal in God's sight, but the business owner has a managerial responsibility (along with a Christian responsibility of treating his/her employee with kindness) and the employee has a responsibility to meet the expectations of his/her employer, working wholeheartedly as if working for the Lord (Colossians 3:23).

As we have previously noted, Paul works *with* and *within* his present culture, aiming his arrows toward Christlike hearts with the end goal of achieving cultural change. His arrows include vocabulary, restrictions, and observations, but his focused target is the heart, not the arrow itself.

In his letter to Rome, Paul boils it down to this: Our culture always needs to submit to God's ways. Paul opens his letter by painting a broad picture of humankind's trajectory away from God; culture is always veering farther off course (Romans 1-2). Anytime individuals refuse to acknowledge God, to thank him, and to submit themselves to his will, they are separated from God and they influence others to do the same. Paul knows that "a little leaven leavens the lump," or "works through the whole batch of dough" (1 Corinthians 5:6; Galatians 5:9). Paul aims to correct errant individuals and groups of individuals, lest their influence affect the entire culture of the church, a culture that should be seeking to be countercultural. How applicable his first-century warning is to us today:

> But God shows his anger from heaven against all sinful, wicked people who suppress the truth by their wickedness. They know the truth about God because he has made it obvious to them. For ever since the world was created, people have seen the earth and sky. Through everything God made, they can clearly see his invisible qualities—his eternal power and divine nature. So they have no excuse for not knowing God.
>
> Yes, they knew God, but they wouldn't worship him as God or even give him thanks. And they began to think up foolish ideas of what God was like. As a result, their minds became dark and confused. Claiming to be wise, they instead became utter fools. And instead of worshiping the glorious, ever-living God, they worshiped idols made to look like mere people and birds and animals and reptiles.
>
> So God abandoned them to do whatever shameful things their hearts desired. As a result, they did vile and degrading things with each other's bodies. They traded the truth about God for a lie. So they worshiped and served the things God created instead of the Creator himself, who is worthy of eternal praise! Amen. That is why God abandoned them to their shameful desires. Even the women turned against the natural way to have sex and instead indulged in sex with each other. And the men, instead of having normal sexual relations with women, burned with lust for each other. Men did shameful things with other men, and as a result of this sin, they suffered within themselves the penalty they deserved.
>
> Since they thought it foolish to acknowledge God, he abandoned them to their foolish thinking and let them do things that should never be done.
>
> Their lives became full of every kind of wickedness, sin, greed, hate, envy, murder, quarreling, deception, malicious behavior, and gossip. They are backstabbers, haters of God, insolent, proud, and boastful. They invent new ways of sinning, and they disobey their parents. They refuse to understand, break their promises, are heartless, and have no mercy. They know God's justice requires that those who do these things deserve to die, yet they do them anyway. Worse yet, they encourage others to do them, too. (Romans 1:18–32 NLT)

But it doesn't have to be this way. Acts 2 shows us what happens when repentance brings a changed heart. A new culture emerges in which Christians call nothing their own and begin to live for others' benefit.

As Paul addresses a big-picture view in Romans 1, he confronts his current culture, calling all disciples to righteousness. Definitions of sin and righteousness (as mentioned in verses 1:18–32) are not negotiable, regardless of culture. (These are defined by Jesus in the gospels as well as by the writers of the letters throughout the New Testament.) Some cultural practices, even practices that work their way into the church, simply don't reflect the heart of Jesus. These practices would include favoritism, treating others as though they are of lesser value, sexual impurity, immorality (heterosexual and homosexual), greed, murder (unborn children or adults), racism, and more. Culture doesn't change overnight, but our hearts and attitudes can decide to change anytime we decide to surrender our will to God's.

When we allow Jesus' teachings to infiltrate and change our hearts, we then begin to view one another differently. Instead of seeing the outward displays of wealth, social status, education, appearance, or ethnicity, we begin to see one another through the lens of Jesus, who looks at the heart rather than the outward appearance. Only then will equality supersede the attitudes of slavery, caste, race, gender, and other forms of discrimination. Paul sums this up in Galatians 3:26–29 as he explains humankind's equal access to salvation:

> So in Christ Jesus you are all children of God through faith, for all of you who were baptized into Christ have clothed yourselves with Christ. There is neither Jew nor Greek, neither slave nor free, nor is there male and female, for you are all one in Christ Jesus. If you belong to Christ, then you are Abraham's seed, and heirs according to the promise.

These words were revolutionary in the culture to which Paul was writing.

Church Culture in Ephesus and Corinth

Let's take a closer look at the first-century culture in Corinth and Ephesus, where two large churches were growing.

Much was happening in the young churches during this time. The world's cultural influences kept creeping—at times leaping—into the church. Since Paul had adopted the heart of Jesus, the desire for all to be saved, he was determined to do all he could to help the young churches shine as lights to the world. In order for this to happen, the church must exhibit the lifestyle and doctrine that God intends. With this in mind, Paul had to address any actions, attitudes, and teachings in the church that might unnecessarily damage the church's reputation in the community at large. Paul strove to point out anything that might distract or hinder the world from seeing Jesus in the church and from recognizing the new changed life that Jesus offered.

Church Culture in Corinth

The church in Corinth was in tough shape, going downhill fast. It was not just struggling to bring together men and women who had been baptized from pagan cultures; it was also grappling with false teachings. Paul, much like a school principal stepping into an out-of-control classroom, knew he must set things in order quickly. A principal going into a chaotic situation must enforce rules quickly and decisively to deal with the problems—perhaps by introducing strict measures like school uniforms and lunchroom silence. The same principal working in a well-ordered school might not need to employ such strict strategies and might be able to focus on bigger-picture issues. But Paul knew that order needed to be established in out-of-order Corinth, and quickly. Paul spoke strongly to the church, and some in Corinth even questioned his authority as an apostle.

> Am I not as free as anyone else? Am I not an apostle? Haven't I seen Jesus our Lord with my own eyes? Isn't it because of my work that you belong to the Lord? Even if others think I am not an apostle, I certainly am to you. You yourselves are proof that I am the Lord's apostle.
>
> This is my answer to those who question my authority.
> (1 Corinthians 9:1-3 NLT)

The Corinthian church had been established after Paul's visit to Macedonia and Athens (Acts 18). Paul had stayed in Corinth for about eighteen months. Early members of the church (including Priscilla and Aquila) had previously been expelled from Rome by the Emperor Claudius. Corinth may have been the first place where Christianity came into contact with a Latin-speaking and predominantly Italian culture. It was current and trendy to adopt Roman culture, and the church was not exempt from this temptation. Ambition and an emphasis on status were being transferred to the church community. The world had infiltrated the church.

Paul became aware of these concerning issues and wrote to this confused church as it tried to find its way in an alien culture. His first letter to Corinth is a response to specific questions raised by the church. Some of these concerns and questions included:

- Divisions in the church (1:10-13; 12:21-25)
- Attraction to worldly philosophy and worldliness (1:18-25)
- Following men instead of Christ (1:11-12; 3:4-9)
- Jealousy and quarreling (3:1-3)
- Arrogance (1:26-31; 3:20-23; 4:18-21)
- Immorality—and being proud of their tolerance of it (5:1-13; 6:15-20)
- Lawsuits among each other (6:1-8)
- Letting their new freedom cause others to stumble—for example, eating food sacrificed to idols (8:9-13)
- Idolatry (10:14-22)

Paul's Teachings on Women

- Drunkenness and greed when taking the Lord's Supper (11:20–22)
- Lack of love (chapter 13)
- Disorder in worship (14:26–40)
- Denying the resurrection (15:12–19)

Paul dealt with moral problems he saw in the church. Roman culture was deeply concerned with appearances and "family values." For several decades, Roman politicians had also striven to devise legislative ways to deal with the perceived social and moral dilemmas. Rules had been put into place to prevent cultural deviances, including rules to keep women "in their proper places." Up until the end of Caesar Augustus' reign in AD 14, rules existed to keep women where they belonged—and to first-century Romans, that place was primarily the home.

These rules of Augustus had included:

- Financial penalties for remaining single
- Rewards for having children (three children gave the father advancement in his political career and gave the mother financial autonomy)
- Dress codes for wives and prostitutes
- Laws forbidding marriage between certain classes
- Penalties against husbands if they ignored their wives' sexual liaisons[29]

These laws attempted to legislate morality, but of course they didn't succeed, since culture and morality begin in the heart, not in rulebooks. This is the environment in which Paul wrote, the environment in which he was trying to help the churches to shine.

Church Culture in Ephesus

In Paul's letters to Timothy, his son in the faith, Paul gives instructions for leading the young church in Ephesus. Paul wrote his first letter to Timothy between AD 62 and 66; he wrote the second from a Roman prison cell around AD 67. Some of the troubling issues and false teachings Paul addresses in these letters regarding the church in Ephesus include:

- Myths, genealogies, speculative intellectualism, controversies, and all kinds of high-sounding nonsense (1 Timothy 1:4, 6–7; 6:20; Titus 3:19)
- Asceticism: laying down special laws (for example, food laws and laws forbidding marriage); listing many things as impure (1 Timothy 4:1–5)
- Failure to provide for one's family (1 Timothy 5:8)
- Greed and gathering money from false teaching (1 Timothy 6:5)
- Denying the coming resurrection (2 Timothy 2:18)
- Quarreling (2 Timothy 2:24–26)
- Men taking advantage of weak-willed women (2 Timothy 3:6–9)
- Gnosticism: the teaching that all matter is evil and the spirit alone is good—thus, the body and spirit can be separated: "If I'm immoral, it's not really me doing it; it's just my body."[30]

And those were just a few of the problems. Paul longed to see the church overcome these wanderings from the truth. False teaching must be stopped. Paul's deepest desire in all he did, in all he wrote, was to see as many as possible be saved.

Although Paul's instructions applied to men and women, some of the heresies taking hold in the church had to do with the role of women. Some of these may have resulted from the widespread cult following of the goddess Artemis.

Ephesus was home to the temple of Artemis. Christianity threatened both the lifestyle and livelihood which stemmed from the worship of this goddess. In Acts 19:23-41 Luke describes the tension and uproar that occur in the city as a result of men and women becoming Christians. This tension shines a glimmer of light into the window of Ephesian culture during Paul's lifetime.

Artemis, the virgin moon goddess, was thought to rule reproduction. Laboring mothers prayed to Artemis for safety during childbirth. Girls between the ages of nine until their marriage were dedicated to Artemis, who was also the ruler of virginity. Her priests were castrated men. Ruling over men, she was said to have killed any man who offended her, including Orion, who claimed to be a better discus thrower than she.[31]

Some of Paul's most misunderstood teachings, found in 1 Timothy 2:8–15, are sandwiched between chapters addressing false teachings in the church. The context sheds light on Paul's instructions, as we will see. His instructions stem from his concern about the church's worldly behavior: If the world could not see Jesus in the church, how could the church save the world? Paul charges Timothy to put an end to false teaching and misrepresentations of the gospel. Again, Paul aims the trajectory of his instructions at a bigger picture. He clearly defines his target as he begins the letter. The aim of his instruction is love:

> But the aim of such instruction is love that comes from a pure heart, a good conscience, and sincere faith. Some people have deviated from these and turned to meaningless talk, desiring to be teachers of the law, without understanding either what they are saying or the things about which they make assertions. (1 Timothy 1:5–7 NRSV)

Shooting the Arrow Through Both Cultures

Paul knows that culture does not become godly through legislation, but rather changes as hearts are transformed to become like Jesus—one individual at a time. In order to reach this target, Paul must get the attention of the Christians whose lives have become blurred with the culture of the world.

As Paul pens these letters, he first shoots his arrow through the urgent issues at hand. He then guides the trajectory so that the ultimate target can be clearly identified and reached. Again, Paul longs for the church to reflect the glory of Christ so that as many as possible can be saved. We can hear his heart through his words as he passionately tells the church:

The View from Paul's Window:

Though I am free and belong to no one, I make myself a slave to everyone, to win as many as possible. To the Jews I became like a Jew, to win the Jews. To those under the law I became like one under the law (though I myself am not under the law), so as to win those under the law. To those not having the law I became like one not having the law (though I am not free from God's law but am under Christ's law), so as to win those not having the law. To the weak I became weak, to win the weak. I have become all things to all people so that by all possible means I might save some. (1 Corinthians 9:19–22)

Addressing Dressing: You Were What You Wore

One of the issues troubling the first-century churches was finding and defining an appropriate way for Christian women to dress. Paul specifically addresses this issue in a letter to Timothy:

> I also want the women to dress modestly, with decency and propriety, adorning themselves, not with elaborate hairstyles or gold or pearls or expensive clothes, but with good deeds, appropriate for women who profess to worship God.
>
> A woman should learn in quietness and full submission. I do not permit a woman to teach or to assume authority over a man; she must be quiet. For Adam was formed first, then Eve. And Adam was not the one deceived; it was the woman who was deceived and became a sinner. But women will be saved through childbearing—if they continue in faith, love and holiness with propriety. (1 Timothy 2:9–15)

How do these instructions connect to the cultural situation of the day, and how should those cultural considerations affect our interpretation and application of the passage today?

Every so often someone may wear a particular article of clothing and hear the remark, "That is so *you!*" Maybe it's the style, maybe it's the color, but usually when we say things like this we are referring to the way clothing reflects a person's personality, not their values. But in first-century Roman culture, it could be said, "You are what you wear."

Clothing distinguished a woman's status and class, and was regulated by law. The *stola* (long tunic) and *vitta* (a ribbon or band worn in the hair) were prohibited for prostitutes; adulterous women were required to wear togas instead of the marriage veil. Legally, if a woman was dressed without a marriage veil, there was no penalty for a man if he had sex with her—consensual or not. Without the protection of the veil, she could not legally claim she had been an unwilling party.[32]

The "adornment" described in 1 Timothy 2:9–15, which was commonplace for the "new woman" as well as the worshippers of Artemis, included ornately braided hair, pearls, gold, and expensive clothing.

The term *adornment* would have resonated with the early Christians to whom Paul was writing. Greek women *adorned* themselves for pagan worship festivals, and young girls called Adorners[33] decorated cult statues:

> It was customary for women in ancient Greek cities to dress up in their "Sunday best" for public worship festivals. Even the cult statues of goddesses were adorned in beautiful clothing at public festivals. At Ephesus, the statue of Artemis was dressed by young girls who held an official title of "Adorner." In contrast to these practices, Paul instructs women to focus their attention not on rich wardrobes, but on the inner beauty of Christian character. As Ignatius of Antioch puts it: "Christians are a new Temple for God, appointed to be shrine-bearers, Christ-bearers, sanctity-bearers, dressed up from head to toe in the commandments of Jesus Christ."[34]

An inescapable link existed between dress codes and personal values. This was the culture in which the first-century church was growing up. Elaborate dress not only depicted values held by the new woman, but also indicated her status, emphasizing wealth and prestige as the focal point of her value. (To put this in modern terms, think of the connotations associated with wearing Coach, Louis Vuitton, and Armani as opposed to thrift shop finds and Walmart brands.)

In the 40s AD, the stoic Seneca (governor of Achaia and a leading statesman during the reign of Nero) wrote to his mother to comfort and praise her:

> Unlike the great majority of women you never succumbed to immorality, the worst evil of our time; jewels and pearls have not moved you; you

never thought of wealth as the greatest gift to the human race; you have not been perverted by the imitation of worse women who lead even the virtuous into pitfalls; you have never blushed for the number of children, as if it taunted you with your years; never have you, in the manner of other women whose only recommendation lies in their beauty, tried to conceal your pregnancy as though it were indecent; you have not crushed the hope of children that were being nurtured in your body; you have not defiled your face with paints and cosmetics; never have you fancied the kind of dress that exposed no greater nakedness by being removed. Your only ornament, the kind of beauty that time does not tarnish, is the great honour of modesty.[35]

These words are significant because they sharply contrast Seneca's mother's modesty with the attitude and lifestyle of other wives of her time. He praises her for possessing a wife's greatest cardinal virtue, modesty (*prudence* in the Greek), a kind of beauty that does not fade or diminish with time.

The two feminine lifestyles—the new woman versus the modest matron—stood in contrast to one another and were even preserved by engravings carved on tombstones. Archaeologists have found tombstones praising discreet women as "self-controlled." Another grave inscription reads, "She did not admire fine clothes, nor gold, when she lived." However, the tombstone of a high-end prostitute as she boasts of her beauty, expensive clothes, and perfume reads: "For all desire me, for I pleased them all."[36] The contrast was stark.

Now let's reread 1 Timothy 2:9–10 in light of these cultural considerations:

> I also want the women to dress modestly, with decency and propriety, adorning themselves, not with elaborate hairstyles or gold or pearls or expensive clothes, but with good deeds, appropriate for women who profess to worship God.

It reads differently now, doesn't it? In light of the cultural times, many scholars agree that the text in 1 Timothy 2:9–15 is cultural and that the transcending message is for Christians to live lifestyles that do not give the world a reason to discredit Christ's message, but rather help to win the world for him.

Some scholars believe that although these teachings may not

make sense in our culture, the instructions are in the Bible and so they still should be applied today. We must decide what we believe—if all of the specific instructions about dress (such as instructions on hairstyles and jewelry) and behavior during worship services were applicable only in the first-century Roman culture or if they were meant to be followed by all Christian women for all time. But the *spirit* of the instructions is transcultural, applicable to Christian women in all times and cultures. And what is that spirit? That Christian women should not seek value and security in their outward appearance, drawing attention to themselves through immodest or pretentious dress, but should instead focus on what matters to God—the heart.

Clothed from the Inside Out

Let's take a look at an important phrase in Paul's instructions:

> I also want women to dress modestly, with decency and propriety, not with elaborate hairstyles or gold or pearls or expensive clothes, but with good deeds, **appropriate for women who profess to worship God.** (1 Timothy 2:9–10, emphasis added)

Public perception of Christian wives was a priority in the church community. Had they dressed like the showy new women, they could have been perceived as high-class prostitutes, followers of Artemis, or women who indulged in worldliness and greed. How quickly such perceptions would have tarnished the young church's reputation!

It might have been tempting for some Christian women in Paul's day to run full-steam ahead with their newfound liberty and equality in the eyes of their loving Father—"In Christ I am free! God does not put me down just because of my gender. We are all equal in Christ: men, women, Greek, Jew, slave, free. In Christ I am free to be me!" But Paul urged them to use that freedom wisely. Given the longstanding culture of the Greek woman, if the women of the first-century church had suddenly broken through the barriers and limitations the previous hundreds of years had imposed upon them—wearing whatever they wanted to wear, speaking boldly whenever and to whomever they wanted to speak—the result would have been to bring dishonor on the church, causing people to say that Christianity was corrupting womanhood.

When Paul's restrictive admonitions regarding women are understood within this cultural and historical context, we can understand his concerns, which in my understanding were for a specific time and situation and were not intended to be viewed and applied in the same way in other cultural contexts and circumstances. Paul's instructions appear to be given for the correction of abuses in a particular situation that threatened the truth of the gospel and the viability of a young church in an antagonistic environment.[37] The transcendent principle standing behind Paul's instructions (in all cultural contexts) is that God wants all to be saved (1 Timothy 2:4; 1 Corinthians 10:33).[37] In other words, disciples of Jesus, who are the church, should always strive to be lights to the world, living in a way that helps as many as possible to see Jesus in their lives.

In any culture, when men and women understand the value given to them by God and shown to them by Jesus, they won't need to seek value anywhere else—not from clothes or money or position or power. Outward transformation begins with the inward transformation of a Christlike heart. Christians are meant to "adorn" ourselves with the internal jewels of the fruits of the spirit. A focus on the external suggests a desire to draw attention to oneself, perhaps to express sensuality or to show off a prominent and wealthy standing in society. We should take care to take the focus off of ourselves, always pointing people to Christ.

Head Coverings and Hairstyles

From clothing to hairstyles...Now let's tackle Paul's instructions on the wearing of veils. While many Christians already consider instructions about veils to be a cultural issue, it's still important to understand *why*. (We will further discuss the relationship between authority and the head in chapter 8.)

Paul writes to the church in Corinth with instructions about hair length and head coverings during prayer:

> I praise you for remembering me in everything and for holding to the traditions just as I passed them on to you. But I want you to realize that the head of every man is Christ, and the head of the woman is man, and the head

of Christ is God. Every man who prays or prophesies with his head covered dishonors his head. But every woman who prays or prophesies with her head uncovered dishonors her head—it is the same as having her head shaved. For if a woman does not cover her head, she might as well have her hair cut off; but if it is a disgrace for a woman to have her hair cut off or her head shaved, then she should cover her head.

A man ought not to cover his head, since he is the image and glory of God; but woman is the glory of man. For man did not come from woman, but woman from man; neither was man created for woman, but woman for man. It is for this reason that a woman ought to have authority over her own head, because of the angels. Nevertheless, in the Lord woman is not independent of man, nor is man independent of woman. For as woman came from man, so also man is born of woman. But everything comes from God.

Judge for yourselves: Is it proper for a woman to pray to God with her head uncovered? Does not the very nature of things teach you that if a man has long hair, it is a disgrace to him, but that if a woman has long hair, it is her glory? For long hair is given to her as a covering. If anyone wants to be contentious about this, we have no other practice—nor do the churches of God. (1 Corinthians 11:2–16)

While a few scholars believe the head coverings discussed in this passage refer to long hair and not to veils, the principles remain the same either way. The veil was two things in Paul's day: a sign of submission and a great protection.

The veil or head covering mentioned in Corinthians had special significance. The Roman bride's wedding veil was a symbol of constancy and lifelong fidelity. It symbolized the husband's authority over his wife. If a married woman failed to wear her head covering, this was a sign that she was withdrawing herself from the marriage and from the Roman law. If a woman did not wish to officially divorce her husband, removing her marriage veil was a symbolic rejection of the marriage. It sent a strong message indicating that a wife was adopting the social morals of the new woman, including promiscuity. A matron, or respectable married woman, would wear a *stola*, a large sleeveless over-garment that was drawn over her head and covered her hair, and a *vitta*, a woolen band for the hair. When a Jewish married woman went outside, she added a face covering to her head-to-floor-length head covering.[38]

A woman caught in adultery would not be allowed to wear the stola or vitta. She would have to wear a plain toga and shave her head in shame. The stola became not only a symbol of honor but also a protection from unwanted attention. This is the background of 1 Corinthians 11. As Paul Zanker writes,

> In the context of social legislation, the stola became a symbol of female virtue and modesty. For the dignified matron, wearing the stola was not only an honor, but a "protection from unwanted attentions."[39]

If we translate verse 10 literally in Greek, it says that a woman ought to retain "her authority upon her head." Sir William Mitchell Ramsay (1851-1939), an archaeologist and New Testament scholar, assumes cultural continuity through the ages as he explains:

> In Oriental lands the veil is the power and honor and dignity of the woman. With the veil on her head she can go anywhere in security and profound respect. She is not seen; it is a mark of thoroughly bad manners to observe a veiled woman in the street. She is alone. The rest of the people around are non-existent to her, as she is to them. She is supreme in the crowd....But, without the veil the woman is a thing of naught, whom anyone can insult....A woman's authority and dignity vanish along with the all-covering veil that she discards.[40]

A more obscure thought on the need to cover a woman's hair stemmed from the teachings of Hippocrates, considered the father of medicine, who died in 370 BC and from whom we get our "Hippocratic Oath". He espoused a theory that lingered for centuries, even into the first century AD. Hippocrates taught that hair was hollow and was part of the reproductive system. Long hair helped women become pregnant by drawing a man's semen upward and inward, since it was hollow and had suction-like qualities. Thus, in this theory a woman's hair was thought to be part of her genitalia. Considering his teaching, it is not surprising that a woman's head was meant to be covered.[41]

Wearing a veil was a cultural necessity for women in Paul's day. In some cultures today, a veil still carries similar connotations and protections. But such is not the case in the Western society in which I (and most of you reading this) live. In Western culture, wearing a veil would not be a protection; rather, it probably would draw unwanted attention. For these reasons, I believe it is no longer prudent for Christian women living in Western cultures to wear a veil.

The Gunaikonomoi Are Watching

Although I have often thought that *gunaikonomos* sounds like a type of reptile, the *gunaikonomos* were actually a type of magistrate widespread in the Greek world by the first century, officials who would enforce moral laws, curb excessive competitive display of wealth, promote female chastity for the sake of fathers and husbands and the gods, and standardize dress in processions.[42] They even enforced the "proper" way for women to grieve publicly, as it was considered improper to be overly emotional in public. Mark Stansbury-O'Donnell describes the role of the *guaikonomos* and the attitude toward grief in first-century Rome:

> Grief and its attendant public behavior were regarded as threatening the order of the city, so that women's participation was generally limited to the *prosethis* inside the house and to laments at the tomb, but only by members of the deceased's family. That such displays were both gender-specific and a threat to the city can be seen in the office of the *gunaikonomos*, who is charged in Solon's law with punishing those who transgressed the statutes....Not only with the behavior of women but also of men in public, especially those who indulge in unmanly and effeminate extravagances of sorrow when they mourn. Mourning is feminine, and for a man to indulge in grief is unmanly and a danger to the social order.[43]

Roman society had strong mores regarding public behavior and appearance. In his first letter to Corinth, Paul recognized that if a Christian woman removed her veil in a public setting, she would appear to be a disreputable woman and her behavior would be considered contentious—the Christian men in the assembly would also be considered contentious (11:4, 16). If, according to Roman law, a woman "was what she wore"—or in this case, what she removed from her head—then removing one's veil made a statement in support of the mores of some of the new wives, who sought to ridicule the much-prized virtue of modesty, which was supposed to epitomize the married woman. Paul reasoned that if a woman took off her veil, it followed that she should also have the shaven, shameful head of an adulterous woman.

Paul felt that it should have been self-evident to the Corinthian Christians that the removal of the veil was totally inappropriate: "Judge among yourselves: is it proper for a woman to pray to God with her head uncovered?" (1 Corinthians 11:13).[44]

"Judge for yourselves" was an emphasis. In Paul's view, it should have been obvious why it was improper: Removing the veil meant that the woman had chosen to adopt the lifestyle and philosophy represented by the new woman.

This would have been obvious to the culture of the time, even though it is not obvious as we look through our window of cultural understanding. The first-century Corinthian Christians probably would have felt Paul's restrictions to be necessary to protect the reputation of the church.

Remember that first-century Corinthian culture was loose and lewd. Society in that day was particularly sensitive when it came to a woman's appearance and public behavior—veils were a hot button issue at that time, so hot that veils warranted special attention by Paul in his letter. But head coverings and public displays of emotion no longer carry the same significance in Western society. Given the cultural considerations, it seems inconsistent to take this passage on head coverings, written to address specific concerns in a specific church for a specific time, and make it universally applicable to all Christian women for all time.

While the passage held great relevance to Corinth at the time, the issue has all but died in modern culture. In my view (and the view of many scholars), Paul's recommendations do not mean that modern Christian women should wear veils (or hats) in church today. In everything he writes, Paul does not lose his big-picture focus: he desires to win as many as possible. The church must be a light, not a hindrance, to this ultimate goal.

Angels Care What I Wear?

> A man ought not to cover his head, since he is the image and glory of God; but woman is the glory of man. For man did not come from woman, but

woman from man; neither was man created for woman, but woman for man. It is for this reason that a woman ought to have authority over her own head, because of the angels. (1 Corinthians 11:8–10)

Because of the angels? Wait, what? Just to add more confusion to an already confusing passage Paul throws in this little zinger: "because of the angels." On this side of eternity, we may never know exactly what Paul meant, but I'll offer several considerations:

1. Paul mentions the angels to show the place, standing, and authority God has given to women. Although women should choose to wear a head covering, submitting to their husbands' honor for the sake of the gospel, they have God-given authority over their own heads—so much authority, in fact, that they will judge the angels:

    Or do you not know that the Lord's people will judge the world? And if you are to judge the world, are you not competent to judge trivial cases? Do you not know that we will judge angels? How much more the things of this life! Therefore, if you have disputes about such matters, do you ask for a ruling from those whose way of life is scorned in the church? I say this to shame you. Is it possible that there is nobody among you wise enough to judge a dispute between believers? (1 Corinthians 6:2–5)

    Just how we are to judge angels Paul does not say, and since that issue is not directly relevant to our study, we can save it for another day. Perhaps Paul is reminding the Corinthian church that since Christians, women and men alike, are one day to be entrusted with the weighty responsibility of judging angels, when it comes to the simple matter of head coverings, surely the women can make responsible choices.

2. Another possible interpretation is that the angels who were watching or serving human women (Hebrews 1:14) could be offended by their lack of responsibility in neglecting proper attire.

3. Another idea espoused by a few scholars traces back to an old rabbinic tradition regarding Genesis 6:1–4:

> When human beings began to increase in number on the earth and daughters were born to them, the sons of God saw that the daughters of humans were beautiful, and they married any of them they chose. Then the LORD said, "My Spirit will not contend with humans forever, for they are mortal; their days will be a hundred and twenty years."
>
> The Nephilim were on the earth in those days—and also afterward—when the sons of God went to the daughters of humans and had children by them. They were the heroes of old, men of renown.

The rabbinic tradition claims that angels were tempted specifically by the beauty of women's long hair, and they then fell prey to the charms of mortal women. Some interpreters see the sons of God as angels who had fallen from their heavenly estate. These fallen angels were then enticed by the women on the earth; they cohabitated with them and produced offspring (half-human, half-angel) called the Nephilim, who then further corrupted the earth so deeply that God was grieved and sent the flood.[45]

4. Another interesting possibility stems from the translation of the word *angels* in this passage.

   Paul says that wives were under obligation to wear the veil because of the "angels." *Angelos* is the Greek word normally translated into English as "angel." Basically, *angelos* means "one who brings a message," and the word can refer to human messengers as well as to the heavenly host—supernatural beings who deliver messages to humans from on high. Translators sometimes struggle to decide when to translate *angelos* as *angel*, meaning "supernatural messenger," or simply as *messenger*, meaning "a human who carries a message." It is possible that the term in 1 Corinthians 11:10 should be translated "messengers."[46] This view makes the most sense to me within the context of these scriptures where Paul is seeking to protect the reputation of the church—but given that scholars can't agree on this, perhaps we will need to ask the angels one day!

That Greek word *angelos* was used not only of those who brought information, but also of those who came to collect information and carry it away to others. Attendance by outsiders and unbelievers was common in Christian gatherings. At times messengers were sent to check up on the meetings to see if the Christians were complying with Roman laws.

Whatever the motive in sending messengers, the report would have gone back to the authorities describing Christian women praying and prophesying in a public setting, activities that would be interpreted in a religious context as being connected to an important priestly office. Remember that women who served as priestesses or worked at temples in Roman culture were often prostitutes. The question would naturally arise: Were these Christian women, so bold in their public worship, the Christian equivalent of pagan temple prostitutes?

Furthermore, if Christian women removed their head coverings while praying and prophesying, this would have signaled that these women identified themselves with the new women who behaved loosely at banquets held in private homes. According to Acts 18:7, private homes were also the setting for Christian gatherings including the Lord's Supper (1 Corinthians 11:17–34). As we will see, it was not unknown for married women to engage in inappropriate conduct in the after-dinners in private homes.

So, if some of the women were not wearing their veils, the messengers could report that the church was full of loose women. This would have prevented the church from shining the bright light of Christ in a dark world.

―――∞∞―――

Many of Paul's arguments seem confusing when taken out of their cultural context. It is often hard for us as contemporary Western readers to remember that cultures elsewhere don't think as we do. And we generally tend to think our viewpoint is the right one! However, when we consider the wide cultural variations across our modern world, including those that relate to women, it should not be too difficult to accept that similar variations abounded in the first-century world.

In the passages we have been exploring, I believe Paul is dealing with social division in the church, addressing specific dilemmas that affected a specific group of people during a specific time in history. His particular instructions about women's behavior and appearance in public worship seem intended to address a problem that eventually faded away as culture shifted over the years.

But that doesn't mean we should throw out Paul's writings and declare them all culturally irrelevant. Paul makes many points that transcend time and culture. Some of those points include not bringing reproach upon one's family or Jesus' church by our personal habits or lifestyles. Numerous scriptures support this principle, and one of the rules of correct interpretation involves exploring all scriptures on a particular subject, also taking into consideration the context in which they were written.

Had Paul been writing a letter to us today he likely would have dealt with different issues and reasoned in a different way. Whatever our culture, we must all ask ourselves whether or not our actions, attitudes, clothing, and words reflect the heart of Jesus, bring honor to his church, and help as many as possible to be saved.

Soap Opera or Scripture? Childbirth, Widows, Deception, and Order

These chapter topics sounds like the plot for a soap opera, right? Let's jump right into the verses containing these plots, twists, and turns.

> A woman should learn in quietness and full submission. I do not permit a woman to teach or to assume authority over a man; she must be silent. For Adam was formed first, then Eve. And Adam was not the one deceived; it was the woman who was deceived and became a sinner. But women will be saved through childbearing—if they continue in faith, love and holiness with propriety. (1 Timothy 2:11–15)

Saved Through Childbirth

I'll start this chapter with childbirth, because certainly anything after childbirth is simpler and less painful (from the viewpoint of one who has given birth multiple times).

In his teachings, Paul consistently drives home a truth: salvation comes from the grace of God and through faith in his Son, not through the performance of functions or duties. In the scriptures, the only kind of birth that brings salvation is our own new birth in which we are raised to new life in Christ (Romans 6:3–6). In 1 Timothy 2:15 Paul is not talking about the salvation of our souls. Women are not saved any differently than men.

We also know that many women, especially in times before modern healthcare, have lost their lives while giving birth. Because they did not live through childbirth, did they not receive salvation?

And what about other women who never became pregnant or bore children at all? Can they not be saved? Obviously, this is not the intended message of Paul's words.

Going back to the values (or lack thereof) held by the new women, one explanation of this passage is that Paul was reassuring Christian women that bearing children is good and right and within God's plan. When Paul wrote this letter to Timothy, who was leading a church in Ephesus, the church was facing the heretical teachings of the new woman, teachings that undermined the value of marriage and childbearing. The new women rebelled against the Greco-Roman culture, which valued women for their contributions in marriage, childbearing, and home management. The new women placed utmost importance upon their physical figures and adornment, and pregnancy and nursing did not enhance their figures. The cultural propaganda of the new woman had captivated some of the women in the church, and they became loud advocates. Their strong voices caused men and women to question and reject some of the culturally accepted norms, such as women bearing children and raising their families. These teachings resulted in fuzzy convictions, arguments, and difficulties for this church full of young Christians living in this particular context and culture. Paul addresses these false teachings in the church in Ephesus. He is once again concerned with the possibility of the gospel being disgraced in the sight of outsiders (1 Timothy 3:7) and with giving the enemy no opportunity for slandering the church (1 Timothy 5:14; 6:1). In Titus 2:3–5 he gives similar instructions to women with the explanation, "so that no one will malign the word of God." Paul's deepest desire in all his teachings is for all to be saved.

Against the false teaching of the day, Paul's words to Timothy may be intended as an affirmation that the natural and beautiful act of childbearing does not keep a woman from full participation in the community of the saved. Thus women would be saved even as they performed the domestic roles traditionally expected of women in their social-historical context (even though those rules were being rejected by the heretical teachings of those who embraced the concept of the new women).[47]

Another plausible explanation stems from the heresies surrounding the worship of Artemis. Women who had worshiped

Artemis (the goddess of childbirth) before becoming Christians would have prayed to her for safety during childbirth. Old habits, though wrong, don't easily die. These new Christian women may have been fearful of danger during childbirth since giving up allegiance to this goddess. Paul may have been reassuring them that Artemis did not hold this power. Artemis was not the Messiah.

Another explanation for "saved through childbirth" is that the reference is not about physical childbirth and women at all, but is about Eve and all those who would later receive salvation because of Jesus' birth. According to this explanation, the word translated "women" in 1 Timothy 2:15 should be translated "she."

And who is the "she"? She is Eve. The previous verses (vv. 13–14) speak of Adam and Eve's deception. So according to this theory, the new translation would read:

> For Adam was formed first, then Eve. And Adam was not the one deceived; it was the woman who was deceived and became a sinner. But **she** will be saved through childbearing—if they continue in faith, love and holiness with propriety.

We read about Adam and Eve's deception in Genesis 3:13, where Eve's sin is followed by God's curse on the serpent. God tells Satan, "I will put enmity between you and the woman, and between your offspring and hers; he will crush your head and you will strike his heel." This curse/prophecy looks ahead to the birth of Jesus and his ultimate victory over Satan.

Proponents of this view state that the word *the* was mistakenly left out of the translation, and 1 Timothy 2:15 should be translated, "she will be saved through *the* childbirth"—that is, the birth of Jesus.

Widows

Another example of cultural context in Paul's writing concerns widows.

> As for younger widows, do not put them on such a list. For when their sensual desires overcome their dedication to Christ, they want to marry.
> Thus they bring judgment on themselves, because they have broken their first pledge. Besides, they get into the habit of being idle and going

about from house to house. And not only do they become idlers, but also gossips and busybodies, saying things they ought not to. So I counsel younger widows to marry, to have children, to manage their homes and to give the enemy no opportunity for slander. Some have in fact already turned away to follow Satan. (1 Timothy 5:11–15)

Circumstances were different in Corinth and in Ephesus. The church in Corinth was in a crisis (see 1 Corinthians 7:26). We do not know the extent of the crisis. Certainly, Paul's preaching was being severely opposed. Perhaps society was changing and in upheaval, or Paul may have sensed impending Christian persecution from the Roman government. Whatever the crisis, in his letter to Corinth, Paul recommended people remain as they were and not marry if they were not already married. But the situation in Ephesus was apparently different. Widows had extra time on their hands and were known to be busybodies, so Paul directed them to get married. Different messages for different contexts.

Remember, Paul's overriding concern throughout his letters was that the church reflect the image of Christ so that more and more could be saved. Therefore, he gave directives addressing the particular issues at hand in order to aim his arrows at the desired target: Christians reflecting the heart of Jesus to the lost world.

Who Lied First?

As I study Paul's teachings, I find it helpful to better understand his personal background along with the background of the culture to which he wrote. As a Pharisee and son of a Pharisee, Paul was a rabbi who had been transformed into a follower of Christ. As a trained rabbi, Paul had "sat at the feet" of his teacher, Gamaliel, who was one of the great rabbinic teachers in first-century Palestine (Acts 22:3). He was greatly influenced by the typical ways rabbis taught.[48] They often used parables, and because their Jewish audiences were generally familiar with the Torah, which they had studied since early childhood, rabbis sometimes stopped a quote or teaching suddenly, with the understanding that the listeners would be able to "fill in the blanks" for themselves.

Paul's Teachings on Women

When addressing matters that were not at the heart of Jesus' teachings, or when giving instructions for particular situations, Paul sometimes used Old Testament texts familiar to him. This was also customary in rabbinical teaching.[49]

All Scripture is inspired by God. This, however, does not prevent Biblical authors from using their distinct writing styles. As author Bruce K Waltke explains, "Inspiration does not bypass the personality of the human author but utilizes his experiences, style, culture, and research."[50]

So let's take a look at Paul's reasoning in 1 Timothy 2:11–15, considering his background as a Pharisee and rabbi. The passage reads:

> A woman should learn in quietness and full submission. I do not permit a woman to teach or to assume authority over a man; she must be quiet. For Adam was formed first, then Eve. And Adam was not the one deceived; it was the woman who was deceived and became a sinner. But women will be saved through childbearing—if they continue in faith, love and holiness with propriety.

Paul instructs women not to teach or to "assume authority over" men because Adam was formed before Eve (v. 13). Paul is referring to the creation account in Genesis 2. Within the synagogue, which provided a model for early church life and structure, male dominance in Jewish culture was traditionally validated by the chronological sequence of creation in Genesis 2: men were created first; therefore men were in charge. (It's interesting to note that in 1 Corinthians 11:8–9 Paul again uses the chronological sequence of Genesis 2 to back up his recommendations that the Corinthian women wear head coverings.)

After stating that Adam was formed first, Paul says the woman was the one who was deceived:

> And Adam was not the one deceived; it was the woman who was deceived and became a sinner. (1 Timothy 2:14)

Were Paul's instructions to women concerning silence, teaching, and authority really a punishment and consequence of Adam being formed first and Eve sinning first?

The restriction on women in this passage uses the argument that Eve was deceived and became a sinner, while Adam was not deceived. Here Paul refers to Genesis 3:13, where scripture tells us that Eve said, "The serpent deceived me and I ate." Because of this, rabbis taught that women were more easily deceived than men. This view of womanhood was widespread in Judaism.[51]

Philo, an Alexandrian Jewish scholar who was a contemporary of Paul's, expressed that since woman "is more accustomed to be deceived than man" and "gives way and is taken in by plausible falsehoods which resemble the truth," the proper relation of a wife to a husband is epitomized in the verb "to serve as a slave."[52]

However, some Jews did acknowledge Adam's full responsibility. Take a look at this account from Edras, a non-canonical historical book traditionally attributed to Ezra:

> O Adam, what have you done? For though it was you who sinned, the fall was not yours alone. (Esdras 7:118)

Paul recognizes Adam's guilt for his own actions. In Romans 5:12 and again in 1 Corinthians 15:21–22, Paul says that Adam, rather than Eve, is responsible for sin's entrance into the world:

> Therefore, just as sin entered the world through one man, and death through sin, and in this way death came to all people, because all sinned. (Romans 5:12)

> For since death came through a man, the resurrection of the dead comes also through a man. For as in Adam all die, so in Christ all will be made alive. (1 Corinthians 15:21–22)

Human nature is tempted to assign blame. Adam and Eve both tried to shift blame to others, but the truth is, they both sinned. In 2 Corinthians 11, Paul points his readers to turn the focus away from Adam's and Eve's deception toward our own tendency to be deceived.

> But I am afraid that just as Eve was deceived by the serpent's cunning, your minds may somehow be led astray from your sincere and pure devotion to Christ. For if someone comes to you and preaches a Jesus other than the

Jesus we preached, or if you receive a different spirit from the Spirit you received, or a different gospel from the one you accepted, you put up with it easily enough. (2 Corinthians 11:3–4)

In this letter Paul uses Eve's deception as an illustration of the possibility that *all* believers in Corinth may be deceived and led away from faith in Christ. And so we see that in two different letters (Ephesians and 2 Corinthians), Paul uses the Eve tradition in differing ways, depending on the problem he is addressing. In both letters, false teaching was at the heart of his concerns.[53]

But wait, Paul is not finished! He goes on to remind his readers that every male emerges from, and therefore is preceded by, a female—and that the origin of male *and* female is in God:

> For as woman came from man, so also man is born of woman. But everything comes from God.
> Judge for yourselves: Is it proper for a woman to pray to God with her head uncovered? (1 Corinthians 11:12)

With this admonition, Paul veers from traditional rabbinic interpretation based on creation chronology and focuses on the *heart* of Genesis 2, that man was incomplete until woman was created, and that God's creation of the female as "one corresponding to [man]" saved the male from his aloneness. As theologian Manfred Brauch puts it,

> In the cultural changes where the influence of the new women was creating disturbances, grasping for authority, rejecting socially accepted roles and espousing heretical teachings, it was natural for Paul to emphasize biblical texts and interpretations that affirmed culturally and religiously accepted female roles, in contrast to the new women who had issued a challenge.
>
> Because women being addressed in Timothy's congregation seem to be among those who "have wandered away" (1 Timothy 1:5) from the faith, and the accompanying Christian lifestyle that shines as a light to the world, Paul's partial use of the Genesis material and its application is understandable. These women, including the young widows, may have been included in Paul's reference in 1 Timothy 5:15 referring to those who "have in fact turned away to follow Satan."[54]

The discussion of "who was created first" and "who was deceived first" takes on even more significance when we understand the previously discussed worship of Artemis. Many scholars believe Paul was addressing a certain heresy brought into the church from the Gentile culture. Theologian Sarah Sumner, in her book *Men and Women in the Church,* notes that the false teachers seem to have been misleading people to follow Satan (1 Timothy 5:15). These teachers were likely stirring up men so that they were more angry than prayerful (1 Timothy 2:8) and tempting the women so that the women were adorning themselves in provocative clothing rather than in good works (1 Timothy 2:9-10). They were allowing women to be loud and argumentative when they sat to learn the false teaching (1 Timothy 2:11). The false teachers were also raising up female false teachers to dominate the men in order to promote the heresy even further (1 Timothy 2:12). 1 Timothy 2:8–14 may have been written to refute the heresies promoted by false teachers in Ephesus.

Sumner continues to explain that when we look back to the culture of first-century Ephesus, we learn from scriptures that the Ephesians were worshipping a goddess. In Acts 19:24–35 we read that Timothy and Erastus were in Macedonia when a riot broke out. (Paul had stayed in Asia.) Demetrius, a silversmith, made shrines for the goddess Artemis. Paul's teachings against idolatry were a threat to business and could ultimately shut down the temple of the goddess Artemis and dethrone her from her majesty.

Luke recounts the angry responses of worshippers of the goddess Artemis, who shouted in unison for two hours, "Great is Artemis of the Ephesians!" Paul, in his instructions for women in 1 Timothy 2, may have been trying to help Timothy to clearly show the Ephesian people that God is not a goddess and Artemis is not the Messiah.[55]

Given the context surrounding the cultural dilemmas, it seems likely that Paul's instruction to women was addressing a particular problem at a particular time, not a permanent hierarchal ordering forced upon us by Eve's sin,

How Silent Is Silence?

Let's tackle another difficult teaching: Paul's exhortation that women should remain silent.

> A woman should learn in quietness and full submission. I do not permit a woman to teach or to assume authority over a man; she must be silent. (1 Timothy 2:11–12)

Some have taken this passage to mean that women cannot ever speak in corporate meetings of the church. Others have taken it to even further extremes, thinking it means that women can't pray aloud in the presence of a man or read scripture in a mixed audience.

A Calm Silence

Let's take a closer look at the words Paul uses in this passage. The Greek word translated "quietness" and "silent" is found several times in the New Testament in both noun and verb form.[56] Note several examples from the NIV:

- 1 Thessalonians 4:11: Make it your ambition to lead a *quiet* (ἡσυχάζω, or "hēsychazō") life, to mind your own business and to work with your hands, just as we told you.[57]

- Luke 23:56: Then they went home and prepared spices and perfumes. But they rested (ἡσυχάζω) on the Sabbath in obedience to the commandment.[58]

- 2 Thessalonians 3:12: Such people we command and urge in the Lord Jesus Christ to settle down (ἡσυχία, or "hēsychia") and earn the bread they eat.[59]

- 1 Timothy 2:12: I do not permit a woman to teach or have

authority over a man; she must be silent (ἡσυχία).⁶⁰

More often the word translated "silent" represents an *attitude* of quietness and does not mean that a person completely refrains from talking. Rooted in the same word, *hesuchyos*, these references carry meanings such as "causing no disturbance to others, tranquility rising from within, keeping one's seat (sedentary), and peaceable."⁶¹ What do all these uses of the word show us? They reveal that the word translated "silent" in 1 Timothy 2 does not mean that a person should not say anything, but instead represents an *attitude* of quietness and mutual submission. For example, when people work together they need to talk, but *the way* they talk to each other is more the subject under discussion. These passages address Christians' tone and attitude in various settings (at work, doing business, or while learning or being taught). Obnoxious, emboldened, "know-it-all" methods of communicating or conducting business don't reflect the attitude of Jesus.

Paul uses the same term for "quiet" in 2 Thessalonians 3:12, which the NIV translates as "settle down." The point is that this term, which is often assumed to mean only verbal silence, is better understood as an indication of a calm, settled, and appropriate attitude.⁶²

Regardless of how the word is intended in these passages, other passages of Scripture make it clear that women weren't expected to be verbally silent in church assemblies. We know that women prophesied and prayed as they assembled (Acts 21:9; Acts 2:17–18; 1 Corinthians 14:5, 31, 39). When Paul encourages quietness, he is more likely addressing the method, attitude, and tone of teaching.

The word translated "silent" in 1 Timothy 2 (ἡσυχία) is different than the word translated as "silent" in 1 Corinthians 14 (σιγάω, pronounced "sigaō"); *sigao* means "not speaking" and will be reviewed in the next section.

Teaching with Authority

Let's take a look at another phrase in 1 Timothy 2:12: "I do not permit a woman to…have authority over a man." The Greek word for "exercise authority," αὐθεντέω (pronounced *authenteō*), is a phrase many scholars believe refers to an abuse or misuse of authority—a domineering spirit. The etymology of the word is associated with violence and abuses of authority.⁶³

In an essay, the late New Testament professor David Scholer, who wrote numerous articles on women and ministry for Fuller Theological Seminary, explains:

> The term translated "to have authority" (*authentein*) occurs only here in the New Testament and was rarely used in the Greek language. It was not the usual word for positive, active authority. Rather, it was a negative term referring to the usurpation and abuse of authority. Therefore, Paul's prohibition in 1 Timothy 2:11–12 is against some abusive activity but not against the appropriate exercise of teaching and authority in the church. The clue to the abuse implied is found within the heretical activity outlined in 1–2 Timothy. The heretics evidently had a deviant approach to sexuality (1 Timothy 4:3; 5:11–15) and a particular focus on deluding women, who were generally (unfortunately) uneducated (2 Timothy 3:6–7).⁶⁴

In addressing these women, Paul, as previously mentioned, may have had in mind the cult of Artemis in Ephesus, where women had seized the role of authority (calling themselves elders) and were running the show. (Remember that Artemis was said to have killed men who disagreed with her.) The context in both 1 Corinthians and 1 Timothy indicates that some Christian women were imitating their worldly peers by becoming overly opinionated and teaching things that were false. As my husband says of one who boldly espouses something they know little about, "Often wrong but never in doubt." Might Paul be advocating a better way—a more godly way? He says that women are allowed to learn as disciples (remember, before Jesus, women were not allowed to be students), in quietness and submission (a rabbinic phrase that was apparently used to describe any good student). However, Paul delineates safe boundaries, clarifying that he is not suggesting that women assume community authority as some pagan women are doing in the shrines.

Paul encourages women to be taught as disciples and coworkers, even pointing out the dangers of withholding learning: uneducated women become easy prey for bad teaching, more easily led astray (2 Timothy 3:6).

Although silence is often the focal point of this verse for modern readers, I believe we may have missed the most important—and most dramatic—message of this scripture. In our concern with questions about silence, have we missed Paul's countercultural proclamation that *a woman should learn*? Remember, in first-century culture, most women did not have the same opportunity to learn as men did. Paul instructed women to learn, and to learn with a humble spirit. What a liberating and exciting opportunity for Christian women, a reflection of Jesus' attitude toward women! Paul welcomes women as learners and warns against adopting the abrasive and domineering attitude of the "new woman" or women who sought to take over the elders' role (as women were doing in the temple of Artemis in Ephesus). It seems Paul's concern is not with insisting that women be completely silent or refrain from teaching altogether; rather, he wants women to learn with a humble, cooperative attitude.

Silence in 1 Corinthians 14

As we mentioned earlier, Paul's first letter to the Corinthians also gives instruction for silence. In 1 Corinthians 14:26–40, Paul addresses the issue of disorderly behavior in the worship assemblies of the Corinthian church. Three different groups are counseled to "hold their peace" or "be quiet" for a while and let someone else speak:

1. Those who speak in tongues should be quiet when there is no one present to interpret.

2. Anyone prophesying when another prophet receives a new message should "stop" and let the second prophet speak.

3. Women (or female prophets or wives of prophets—both are alternate translations) who want to question their husbands should be quiet in church and ask their questions at home.

The Greek word σιγάω (sigaō) is used in all three instances, but most English translations, including the NIV, say, "women should remain silent in the churches." Unfortunately, this rendering communicates an unequivocal command for all time and situations. The Greek text clearly did not mean this, given other scriptures that shed light on Paul's teachings.[65]

But let's take a look at the NIV rendering of this entire passage:

> Two or three prophets should speak, and the others should weigh carefully what is said. And if a revelation comes to someone who is sitting down, the first speaker should stop. For you can all prophesy in turn so that everyone may be instructed and encouraged. The spirits of prophets are subject to the control of prophets. For God is not a God of disorder but of peace—as in all the congregations of the Lord's people.
>
> Women should remain silent in the churches. They are not allowed to speak, but must be in submission, as the Law says. If they want to inquire about something, they should ask their own husbands at home; for it is disgraceful for a woman to speak in the church. (1 Corinthians 14:29–35)

Earlier in the same chapter (verse 5), Paul writes,

> I would like every one of you to speak in tongues, but I would rather have you prophesy. The one who prophesies is greater than one who speaks in tongues, unless someone interprets, so that the church may be edified. (1 Corinthians 14:5)

Paul has already indicated in this letter to the Corinthians that women did participate in prayer and prophesy in the church (1 Corinthians 11:5, 10; 14:3–5). This fact alone shows that 1 Corinthians 14:34–35 cannot be a general, absolute, and timeless prohibition against women speaking in church. Acts 2:17 also states that women prophesied in the early church, and we know that Philip's four unmarried daughters prophesied (Acts 21:9).

The general meaning of prophet is: a person (male or female) who expounded upon the Word of God for the enlightenment and edification of their hearers.

Given that women clearly did participate verbally in the worship, the silence Paul mentions in 1 Corinthians 14:34–35 must be a specific, limited silence. Numerous suggestions have been offered, and I'll just share a few of them.

1. Silence when speaking in tongues

One view suggests that the speaking Paul prohibits is speaking in tongues, since tongue-speaking, or *glossolalia*, is frequently mentioned in the preceding context (1 Corinthians 14). However, *glosso-*

lalia is always referred to as "tongues" or "speaking in tongues" and never simply as "speaking."⁶⁶ And Paul's prohibition in 1 Corinthians 14:34 uses the word *laleo* (meaning "to utter a voice or emit a sound; to speak"),⁶⁷ not *glossolalia*, making this view unlikely.

2. Silence in judging prophecy

Another view, espoused by some who oppose women speaking with authority in the church, is to identify the specific kind of speaking prohibited with the judgment of the prophets mentioned in 1 Corinthians 14:29: "Two or three prophets should speak, and the others should weigh carefully what is said."

This view argues that women may prophesy (1 Corinthians 11:5) but may not judge or evaluate prophecy. The evaluation of prophecy is the authoritative level of speech in the church from which women are to be excluded.

This view is problematic, however. First, the definition of the word "speak" in 1 Corinthians 14:34 contains no implication that would support identifying it with the concept of prophetic evaluation; such a connection cannot even be found within the immediate context (14:34–35). Second, the idea of the church having two levels of speech—prophecy and the judgment of prophecy—with the understanding that judgment of prophecy is the highest level and is reserved for men alone—is not stated or supported by other Pauline teachings. In fact, Paul's definition of prophecy (1 Corinthians 14:1–25) implies that prophecy itself is the highest level of authoritative speech in the church.⁶⁸

3. Silence in public worship

Another interpretation holds that there are two kinds of worship in chapters 11 and 14. In chapter 11, women pray and prophesy alongside the men during private or informal worship. Their prophecy is what we today might call "testimony" or "sharing." The argument suggests that in chapter 14, the worship is more structured. It may be like the synagogue worship (Luke 4:16–21; Acts 13:5), where one person is invited to bring the main exhortation. In this view, during public worship a few others may also speak, but none of them may be women.

But this view does not adequately harmonize 1 Corinthians

14:26 and 14:35. How can Paul say everyone has a hymn or word of instruction in 14:26 and also say women must be silent in 14:35 without providing a qualification or limit on that silence? It seems clear to me that Paul anticipated that women would be speaking in some way during worship (both public and private) and that he did not expect total silence from women.

4. Silence sometimes

Yet another option harmonizes 14:26 and 14:35 by proposing a limit on the command of silence in 14:35. Specifically, when Paul says women must remain silent, he means they must be silent *during the testing of prophecy*. The testing of prophecy is the theme of 14:29–35. Paul wanted women to use their gifts, but he also wanted all teaching to be tested. That task belonged to elders (also called overseers), especially teaching elders. In this view, close analysis of 1 Corinthians 14 supports the view that women may prophesy (11:5) but must remain silent when prophesy is tested.[69]

5. Silence for keeping order

Order in worship was required by men as well as women. "Silence" was expected from all at different times, to keep order in the church (1 Corinthians 14:28–29). If no interpreter was available, men and women were to pray in tongues only to themselves and God, and prophets were to restrict their own speech voluntarily if another arose with a message from God.

It seems plausible that the speech prohibited here for women refers only to disruptive questions that wives (who were usually uneducated in the culture of Paul's time, through no fault of their own) were asking their husbands. This corresponds precisely with the resolution Paul offers in 1 Corinthians 14:35: "If they want to inquire about something, they should ask their own husbands at home." Such disruptive questioning was also considered a disgrace in Paul's day, when it was widely believed that it was morally indiscreet for any wife to say anything on any subject in public. This view of disruptive questioning also fits well with the specific context (1 Corinthians 14:26–40): Paul is concerned about appropriateness and order, which permit genuine edification (note that 1 Corinthians 14:26 expects everyone, male and female, to participate in worship).[70]

The early church often met in homes, with men and women sitting on opposite sides of the room. Questions and comments would have been shouted in order to be heard. Perhaps the women were inquiring about the meaning of the ecstatic or prophetic utterances, thereby contributing more noise to an already chaotic assembly. It seems the setting was a bit wild and disorderly, a scene we have a hard time picturing through our modern Western churchgoing eyes. Order in the assembly (although we have seen that their disorder looked different than ours) seems to be the principle being addressed, and this principle (the need for orderliness and a lack of interruption), spans cultures and time.

Silence and Synagogue Procedures Concerning Sexual Innuendos

Paul's instructions might have been influenced by synagogue procedures (or perhaps laws) where women took no active role. Remember, the synagogue was a man's world; the home was the woman's world.

The Mishnah (the first written record of the oral law) disallowed women's participation in the synagogue because their sexual appeal to men could lead to social disruption.

The Talmud (Jewish writings that include both the Mishnah and rabbinic commentary on scripture and Jewish law) also restricts women's participation in the synagogue. The Talmud says, "The voice of a woman is indecent." (BT *Berakhot* 24a). This line is part of a ruling that a man may not recite the *Shema* while he hears a woman singing since her voice might divert his concentration from the prayer.

Such teachings and traditions certainly could have been the backdrop for the regulations and views given to the church on the woman's role in the public assembly.

Silence and Attitude

Christian women who prophesied, spoke in tongues, and interpreted prophesy were teaching men in the congregation when they did so (considering the definitions of prophesying and interpreting). Perhaps Paul's words in 1 Corinthians 14 were a correction directed toward overbearing women who caused chaos in the church. We have learned that some women sought to "take over," or speak boldly on things they knew nothing about, creating disorder in the service. While commanding "complete silence" would have solved the immediate problem of disorder, we know that in the big picture Paul encouraged a heart of humility and a "quiet spirit." If the heart is not addressed, the outward rules become mere place-keepers, for as Jesus taught in Luke 6:45, the mouth speaks from the overflow of the heart.

Cultural Practices or Timeless Principles?

If we conclude that these instructions were cultural practices, what would this mean for women in the church today? Is it consistent when we call women to remain silent in worship for all time, but do not also insist that women continue to prophesy and speak in tongues? We might ask, since Paul gives instructions on three topics—tongue-speaking, prophesying, and women speaking—all in a single passage, and our fellowship considers the first two issues to be first-century matters no longer applicable in the same way to Christians today, should we not consider *all three issues* to be cultural and time-sensitive?

I teach the Bible and conduct workshops all over the world, most commonly on the topic of how Jesus helps us to deal with issues of loss, rejection, trust, control, and identity. At times men have asked if they could attend my workshops. In years past I have responded by saying I didn't feel comfortable with their presence—I felt it was inappropriate for me to teach men because I would be exercising an unbiblical authority over them. I felt this way because of my cultural background. But now, after studying women's roles so extensively, I feel differently and would personally welcome any man who wished to take part in a workshop I teach (though I would honor the viewpoint of my leaders or the leaders of the church I was visiting if they did not feel comfortable with this arrangement). I am confident in my conscience and understanding of the scriptures that I am not taking over any authority simply by teaching a coed audience.

What would constitute taking over male authority? A brief summary would be this: If I attended a workshop, class, sermon, or other setting where a man was teaching and I interrupted him, corrected him, publicly insulted his grammar usage, and questioned his right to teach, that would be taking over authority. My behavior would be similar to what the women were doing in 1 Corinthians 14. (I believe it would also be disrespectful if a man did such things when a woman was teaching.) At the heart of these issues are the Bible's instructions on how we are to treat one another and how all disciples of Christ must develop the selfless, humble attitude of Christ—no matter our gender.

Summary: Always and Forever or a Moment in Time?

We must question whether Paul's instructions concerning women, authority, silence, and head coverings were intended to lay down permanent laws of practice for our churches, or if they were instead intended to deal with pertinent, timely, cultural issues.

If we view all of Paul's more practical advice in 1 Corinthians 14 and 1 Timothy 2 as being specific to a particular time and culture (again, these chapters include instructions about tongue-speaking, prophesy, women's participation and dress, and general worship guidelines), and if we consider his instructions on tongue-speaking and miraculous gifts to be obsolete today because they address issues that died with the time, then we must determine whether his advice about women is also obsolete. In my view it would seem inconsistent if some instructions were intended for a particular moment in time, addressing specific issues and concerns that no longer exist, while other instructions in the same passages were still applicable.

In my view, Paul's instructions were written in order to calm the chaos of the first-century church, address false teaching, and to encourage respectful, mutually submissive attitudes (rather than abrasive and disrespectful behavior) so that the church might shine as a light to the world. Disruption and interruption certainly would dim that light, given the culturally accepted practices of the day. Thus, Paul's prohibitive instructions would appear to be cultural, time-sensitive instructions addressing the lifestyles of young churches.

It seems significant that, after Paul addresses the troubling issues at hand (the covering of a woman's head, the uncovering of a man's head, and inappropriate practices during the Lord's Supper), Paul does not end his letter here, but continues into chapters 12 and 13. Had Paul ended his letter to the Corinthians with chapter 11, we might be left to focus on the arrows of regulations and corrections about corporate worship. Instead, Paul follows the trajectory of these arrows toward a "more excellent way" (1 Corinthians 12:31). I can almost feel the crescendo in Paul's passion as he tells the Corinthians, "And yet I will show you the most excellent way." In the famous passage on love, 1 Corinthians 13, Paul expands his focus from the specific to the general, describing the transcending principles of love, selflessness, humility, and unity—the overall aim of his instruction (1 Timothy 1:5).

Focus on the Target More than the Arrow

Are we suggesting we should just ignore 1 Corinthians 14? Write the whole thing off as outdated and irrelevant? Of course not. While some of the specific practices may no longer apply, the *values* transcend time and culture, and they remain. The big-picture attitude and environment God wants in his church is the same today as it was then. The attitudes of Jesus—humility, submission, love, respect, mutual concern—must be implanted and formed in our hearts. The ways we treat one another are of utmost importance. Today's church must demonstrate a culture of love and respect, reflecting the changed values of those who have become Christians—those who have renounced the culture of the world and had their lives transformed by the cross of Christ.

In 1 Corinthians 12:12–13 Paul closely repeats the statement he also made in his letter to the Galatian church (Galatians 3:26–27) describing God's view of community and oneness:

> Just as a body, though one, has many parts, but all its many parts form one body, so it is with Christ. For we were all baptized by one Spirit so as to form one body—whether Jews or Gentiles, slave or free—and we were all given the one Spirit to drink.

Then in 1 Corinthians 13, Paul goes on to beautifully describe the attitude of love that should rule the way we treat one another: "Love is patient, love is kind. . . ."

Once more Paul's overarching goal, the aim of his arrows in these verses, is his desire for all to be saved and the church to be strengthened. Like the first-century Corinthians, we must do all we can to strengthen the church. The church is to be a light to the world so that anyone who comes into a worship service will know that Christ is among us. Paul stated as much when he described the purpose for the first-century believers' prophesying:

> But if an unbeliever or an inquirer comes in while everyone is prophesying, they are convicted of sin and are brought under judgment by all, as the secrets of their hearts are laid bare. So they will fall down and worship God, exclaiming, "God is really among you!" (1 Corinthians 14:24–25)

Although in our fellowship we do not gather to exercise our gifts of public prophesy and tongue-speaking, our overall goal is the same: to show the power of God to an unbelieving world through our love for each other and our worship assemblies.

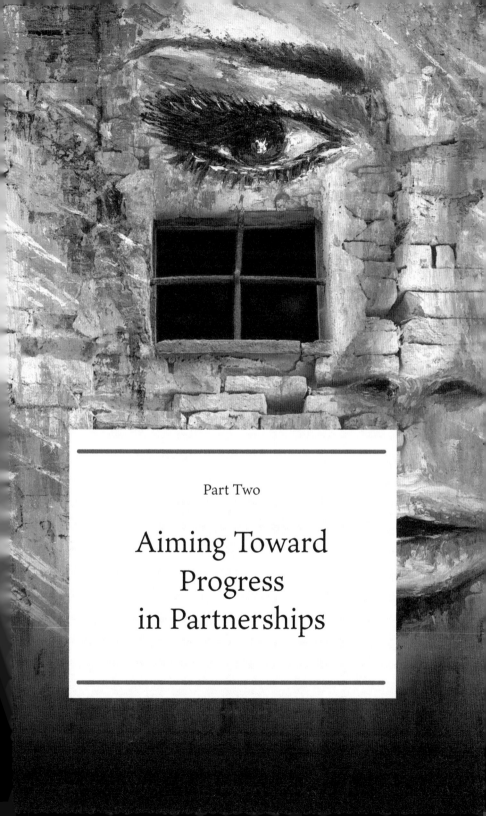

Part Two

Aiming Toward Progress in Partnerships

9

Unity and Partnership in Ephesians 5

As Paul looked out from his window upon his culture's views of marriage and parenting, he likely witnessed eroded, ungodly values. When we read Ephesians 5 through the window of our modern culture, it is impossible to comprehend how radical Paul's instructions to families in Ephesians 5 were in his day. Paul championed a new way of thinking about marriage, a new way for spouses to treat one another. The Christian view of marriage is broadly accepted today, but in Paul's day this was not the case. Remember that in Paul's Jewish culture a woman was considered property: she was without legal rights, a husband's possession to do with as he willed. Divorce was tragically common and easy to obtain.

Though rabbis held a high *ideal* of marriage, general Jewish practice fell far short of the ideal.

Two famous first-century rabbis debated the acceptable reasons for divorce. The stricter rabbis, headed by the Rabbi Shammai, held that the phrase "indecency" (which gave cause for divorce) meant adultery and adultery alone. The more liberal rabbis, headed by the equally famous Hillel, interpreted the phrase in the widest possible way. They said that it meant that a man might divorce his wife if she spoiled his dinner by putting too much salt in his food, if she walked in public with her head uncovered, if she talked with men in the streets, if she spoke disrespectfully of her husband's parents in her husband's hearing, if she was a brawling woman, if she was troublesome or quarrelsome. Another rabbi, Akiba, interpreted the phrase "if she finds no favor in his eyes" to mean that a husband might divorce his wife if he found a woman whom he considered more attractive.[71]

Another, more intermediate view on divorce during this time was from Instone-Brewer, namely that a violation of one's wedding vows constitutes grounds for divorce.[72]

Not surprisingly, companionship and fellowship in marriage were rare. In Paul's Greco-Roman culture divorce was thought to be rampant and fidelity nearly non-existent.

Life was also difficult for children. In this patriarchal culture the father had absolute power over his family. He could sell his children as slaves or punish them at will. His authority remained over his children after they became adults.

In a letter dated 1 BC from a man named Hilarion to his wife, the husband—who had traveled to Alexandria—wrote his wife, Alis, about home matters:

> Hilarion to Alis his wife heartiest greetings, and to my dear Berous and Apollonarion. Know that we are still even now in Alexandria. Do not worry if when all others return I remain in Alexandria. I beg and beseech you to take care of the little child, and, as soon as we receive wages I will send them to you. If—good luck to you!—you bear offspring, if it is a male, let it live; if it is a female, expose it. You told Aphrodisias, "Do not forget me, How [sic] can I forget you? I beg you therefore not to worry." The 29th year of Caesar, Pauni 23.[73]

In a similar vein, Hilarion's contemporary Seneca writes, "We slaughter a fierce ox; we strangle a mad dog; we plunge the knife into sickly cattle lest they taint the herd; children who are born weakly and deformed we drown."[74]

Lynn Cohick, in her book *Women in the World of the Earliest Christians*, gives us a further glimpse into history:

> The philosophical stance, that male was superior to female, played itself out in the cultural arena where women as a group were inferior to men. Moreover, this position played a key role in the social configuration of the ideals of marriage. From classical Greece up through the reign of imperial Rome, the subordination of women was understood as a moral issue, although it was also enforced by social and legal codes.[75]

A half-century before Paul, Plato shaped many of the ideals of marriage that persisted for centuries. He taught that the family is the smallest unit of social organization, where the husband rules his family (wife, children, slaves) as a king rules his colony. Although he states that the husband rules his wife in a constitutional position, he then qualifies his apparent movement toward equality with the explanation that "the inequality is permanent."[76]

Plato's philosophy continued into the second century AD as Soranus of Ephesus (a leading physician) taught, "The female is by nature different from the male, so much so that Aristotle and Zenon the Epicurean say that the female is imperfect, the male, however, perfect."[77]

Cohick continues,

> Also from the second century AD, Plutarch continues to affirm the value of marriage. In this work he offers further examples of a proper wife.... Eschewing fancy clothes and remaining silent in public reveal her noble character. In the bedchamber she should show her affection and modesty in lovemaking. She must accept her husband's extramarital sexual activities with good grace and not let such behaviors push her toward divorce....The husband may enjoy sex with others (except married women), but should avoid provoking his wife to jealousy. Plutarch reaches beyond the legal codes when he suggests that married couples have one purse, under the husband's control even if the wealth comes from the wife.[78]

While we can't glean a complete picture of first-century culture, glimpses like these help us to better understand the environment in which Paul wrote—the problems and pitfalls he was attempting to correct. And so it is in this first-century family culture that Paul writes,

> Submit to one another out of reverence for Christ.
> Wives, submit yourselves to your own husbands as you do to the Lord. For the husband is the head of the wife as Christ is the head of the church, his body, of which he is the Savior. Now as the church submits to Christ, so also wives should submit to their husbands in everything.
> Husbands, love your wives, just as Christ loved the church and gave himself up for her to make her holy, cleansing her by the washing with water through the word, and to present her to himself as a radiant church, without

stain or wrinkle or any other blemish, but holy and blameless. In this same way, husbands ought to love their wives as their own bodies. He who loves his wife loves himself. After all, no one ever hated their own body, but they feed and care for their body, just as Christ does the church—for we are members of his body. "For this reason a man will leave his father and mother and be united to his wife, and the two will become one flesh." This is a profound mystery—but I am talking about Christ and the church. However, each one of you also must love his wife as he loves himself, and the wife must respect her husband. (Ephesians 5:21–33)

Children, obey your parents in the Lord, for this is right. "Honor your father and mother"—which is the first commandment with a promise— "so that it may go well with you and that you may enjoy long life on the earth."

Fathers, do not exasperate your children; instead, bring them up in the training and instruction of the Lord.

Slaves, obey your earthly masters with respect and fear, and with sincerity of heart, just as you would obey Christ. Obey them not only to win their favor when their eye is on you, but as slaves of Christ, doing the will of God from your heart. Serve wholeheartedly, as if you were serving the Lord, not people, because you know that the Lord will reward each one for whatever good they do, whether they are slave or free.

And masters, treat your slaves in the same way. Do not threaten them, since you know that he who is both their Master and yours is in heaven, and there is no favoritism with him. (Ephesians 6:1–9)

The Bible calls for a different dynamic and relationship. Children are to honor and obey parents. Parents have authority (though the scriptures also call for parents to nurture and train their children without exasperating them). Without parental authority, children will not learn consequences and rewards for right and wrong and for safe living. However, unlike the culture of Paul's day, the Bible makes it clear that even parental authority has limits. Paul reminds fathers not to exasperate their children (Ephesians 6:4). Exasperation often happens when parent-child relationships don't change from authoritative interactions when children are young to respectful connection, persuasion and reasoning as children mature into young adulthood.

Submission and Laying Down Your Life

The Ephesians passages here begin with a command to mutual submission. Paul then describes how each person is to practice their submission in their treatment of one another.

For the first-century audience it was not the wife material that was radical or strange; it was the husband material.[79] It's interesting to note the imbalance between the imperatives Paul uses for each gender. Paul commands wives to submit. However, he does not command husbands to rule or to lead (the reciprocal commands one might expect in contrast to *submit*); rather, he calls husbands to *love*. The husband's rule or authority is assumed in the discussion, but is softened considerably through Paul's emphasis on love and his use of sacrificial imagery. In this way, Paul upholds the status quo for women; however, he pushes the boundaries for men with the direction of his command.[80]

If I could be a first-century Christian man, looking over Paul's shoulder as he writes instructions on family relationships (and of course I can only use my imagination here!), I wonder what kind of fearful responses I might have to Paul's instructions because of my culture, expectations, and experience: *If you ask me to sacrifice myself for my wife, she will take over. If you ask me to consider my slaves as brothers and equals, they will no longer work for me. If you take away my authority over my adult sons by asking them to leave father and mother and be joined to their wife, they will no longer honor me.* Paul, in his instructions, stretches the understanding of the status quo. He recasts hierarchal relationships, pointing the young churches toward a better (more Christlike) way of functioning together.

If we refer back to the hermeneutics we described in chapter one, what might we learn? What was the cultural situation in the first century concerning marriage and submission? How should this passage be understood in light of the larger principles of the gospel? Where are the implications of the kingdom of God taking us? Questions to ponder.

In both Ephesians and Colossians Paul affirms master/slave relationships at the same time that he discusses husbands and wives. We understand that Paul recognized the cultural mores of his time while aiming his arrow toward the timeless principles of his target:

humility, mutual respect, love, and self-sacrifice. These are the qualities that can change a culture one life at a time.

In Ephesians 5:21–24, Paul expresses himself to an audience in which husbands are already in a position of authority over wives. Would he have addressed the relationship differently in another culture? We don't know the answer, and scholars cannot agree.

Meanings for "Head"

At the focal point of the questions concerning authority in Ephesians 5 is the word translated "head" in verse 23: "For the husband is the head of the wife as Christ is the head of the church, his body, of which he is the Savior." Scholars (most with the initials PhD or ThD after their names) disagree on Paul's intended meaning of the word.

I will briefly summarize the most common views on the meaning of "head" (the Greek word *kephale*) as it is used in Ephesians 5:23:

- When head is translated from Greek (again, the Greek word is kephale), the word does not suggest a chain of command or a sense of hierarchy. If the word was intended to mean "one having authority," another Greek word (*archon*) would have been used. Well-known scholars arguing for this meaning are Gordon Fee, Phillip Payne, and Berkeley and Alvera Mickelson.

- The word *kephale* means something more resembling "source," using the reasoning that women and men are derived from each other, mutually dependent in the Lord. Gilbert Bilezikan and Catherine Kroeger are known for their arguments in favor of this meaning. Andrew Perriman holds a similar view, though he would use the word "beginning" instead of "source."

- In contrast, some other scholars argue that *kephale* means "ruler over" and clearly denotes a hierarchal structure of authority. They discount the validity of the interpretation of *kephale* as "source" and believe the word carries a meaning of authority. Wayne Grudem and John Piper are well known for espousing this viewpoint.

Rather than detailing the helpful but tedious reasoning that led these scholars to their opinions, at the end of this book I have referenced an article that does an excellent job of conveying the various schools of thought. Although the author, theologian Alan Johnson, states his viewpoint at the beginning, he seeks to present an unbiased description of the main arguments used by the most widely recognized scholars on the subject. He presents these studies in chronological order of their appearance on the debate scene. See the Notes section for a link to his article, "A Meta-Study of the Debate over the Meaning of "Head" (*Kephalē*) in Paul's Writings."[81]

While some believe the scripture in Ephesians 5 gives a clear description of hierarchy and leadership (a complementarian relationship), others believe Ephesians 5 describes mutual submission without hierarchy (an egalitarian relationship).

In short, the complementarian believes that the Bible establishes male authority over women, making male leadership the biblical standard. According to this view, God calls women to submit to male leadership and take up supportive roles to their husbands and male leaders in the church. Opinions are split over whether this hierarchy extends outside the church to the public sphere.

Egalitarians believe leadership is not determined by gender but by the gifting and calling of the Holy Spirit, and that God calls all believers to submit to one another. At the heart of debate is whether God has placed limits on what women can or can't do in the home and in the church—and, by extension, into other spheres of life (for example, work, community influence, and government). A core scripture seen by egalitarians as promoting their view is Galatians 3:23–29, which egalitarians say transcends the old law and fulfills the spirit of Jesus:

> Before the coming of this faith, we were held in custody under the law, locked up until the faith that was to come would be revealed. So the law was our guardian until Christ came that we might be justified by faith.
>
> Now that faith has come, we are no longer under a guardian.
>
> So in Christ Jesus you are all children of God through faith, for all of you who were baptized into Christ have clothed yourselves with Christ. There is neither Jew nor Gentile, slave nor free, nor is there male and female, for you are all one in Christ Jesus. If you belong to Christ, then you are Abraham's seed, and heirs according to the promise.

So how should we interpret Paul's often confusing mix of egalitarianism and hierarchical complementarianism? I believe we first must gain conviction about the transcending principles. Some of these are:

- Submission to one another is the high calling of all Christian relationships.
- Domineering and harsh uses of authority are ungodly.
- Love and respect are to be given to all.
- Leadership is to be selfless and servant-like.
- Spouses are "one flesh," so the way they treat each other affects them both.
- All Christians comprise one body in Christ, so the way disciples treat each other affects the body as a whole.

The Head and Body Metaphor

Metaphors paint pictures. Jesus used metaphors to describe himself. In the gospel of John we are introduced to Jesus as bread, living water, the gate, the vine, the light, and the shepherd. These pictures help us understand some of the beautiful, life-giving, and loving characteristics and qualities of Jesus. We understand these to be pictures and so we don't argue over what kind of bread Jesus is—unleavened, whole wheat, or rye. We understand from this metaphor that he fills our spiritual hunger and is our sustenance for spiritual survival.

Too often, I believe, we attempt to dissect meanings in metaphors that were not intended to be dissected—for example, by straining through the definitions of "head" mentioned in the previous section.

In Ephesians 5:23 Paul uses the metaphors of the husband as head of the wife and Christ as head of the church:

> Submit to one another out of reverence for Christ.
> Wives, submit yourselves to your own husbands as you do to the Lord.
> For the husband is the head of the wife as Christ is the head of the church,
> his body, of which he is the Savior. (Ephesians 5:21–23)

In these two verses Paul addresses two different relationships: husbands with wives and Christ with the church. In verses 30–32 he takes us to a focal point:

> For we are members of his body. "For this reason a man will leave his father and mother and be united to his wife, and the two will become one flesh." This is a profound mystery—but I am talking about Christ and the church. (Ephesians 5:30–32)

The metaphor of head and body for the marriage relationship paints a powerful picture of unity—one flesh. Thus, marriage is not meant to be separated (decapitated). Let's take a look at several significant commonalities and differences in these comparisons. (Note that I am using "head" as it is most often translated—as a reference to the appendage that sits on top of our neck.)

A head cannot function without a body and a body cannot function without a head. The two are meant to be united. The church has no function without Christ—it would have no purpose.

The church is dependent on Christ for its existence. He redeemed us as individuals and made us part of the church, his body. Christ is dependent on the church, for without the church his mission cannot be fulfilled. This concept is reflected in Paul's words in Colossians 1:24: "Now I rejoice in what I am suffering for you, and I fill up in my flesh what is still lacking in regard to Christ's afflictions, for the sake of his body, which is the church."

We might ask, *What could possibly be lacking from Christ?* Only one thing is lacking: the taking of his message of reconciliation to all the world. Thus, Christ is dependent on his body, the church, to spread this message and to show this dark world Jesus' power to change lives.

While Jesus (our head) offers us salvation, the same is not true in the marriage relationship. The husband is not the savior of the wife—only Jesus saves.

In 1 Corinthians 7:3, when Paul discusses the physical bodies of husband and wife in the sexual relationship, he says that they should fulfill each other's sexual needs. In the next verse he states,

> The wife does not have authority over her own body but yields it to her husband. In the same way, the husband does not have authority over his own body but yields it to his wife. (1 Corinthians 7:4)

Paul makes it clear that in the sexual relationship, each spouse willingly gives their authority over their bodies to their spouse. The wife's body does not "belong" to her husband any more than the husband's body "belongs" to the wife—they belong to each other.

It's important to acknowledge the differences in these metaphors. The marriage metaphor cannot be extrapolated to mean exactly the same thing as Christ being the head of the church because the husband is not the wife's savior, and the husband and wife must yield the authority of their own body to their spouse.

The kind of "headship" indicated for marriage in these scriptures seems to be different from the traditional hierarchal dynamic that often comes to mind (at least it is different from the dynamic I am familiar with from my cultural background). Paul defines "headship" in a selfless and sacrificial way, a way that is strikingly different from the kind of relationship that would have been understood in his long-held hierarchal culture.

While Jesus was given all authority, the scriptures never portray Christ as one who "lords his authority" over the church. Instead, Jesus' life reflects the absolute submission of his own will in order to bring salvation to his beloved bride, the church.

Unity: A Profound Mystery

Scholar Alice Matthews offers an explanation of *kephale* as painting a picture rather than giving a definition:

> We must be clear about what we can and cannot say about *kephalē*, "head." The Bible simply states that the husband is "head of the wife" analogous to Christ as head of the church in his role as its Savior....If we ask what this means, theologian Sarah Sumner responds, "Scripture doesn't tell us definitively. It tells us what it looks like—self-sacrifice. Thus we have a picture, not a definition."

How can two become one? The mystery of marriage is that two (head and body) become "one flesh." Sumner writes the following: "When head is defined as 'leader' and body is defined as 'helper,' the biblical mystery is lost. What is mysterious about a leader coupled up with his helper? Not very much. Nor is it particularly inspiring. But it is altogether breathtaking to see the biblical picture of body and head joined mysteriously as one . . . The picture of 'one flesh'. . .indicates immediately the organic unity that bonds a husband and wife."[82]

Theologian Sarah Sumner continues this thought.

> It is not so disturbing to imagine a leader breaking up with his assistant. But it is utterly disconcerting to imagine a body being amputated physically from its head....A body belongs to its head and a head belongs to its body. That's why God hates divorce. The husband as "head" is analogous to Christ as head of the church and as savior of the body. *Giving himself* for the body? That is far from emphasizing rule or authority.[83]

According to the Bible, marriage is about two people joined indissolubly as "one flesh." Paul wasn't kidding when he stepped back from what he had written and said, "This is a profound mystery." We must take it for that. Let's go down a few verses to where Paul writes:

> For this reason a man will leave his father and mother and be united to his wife, and the two will become one flesh." This is a profound mystery—but I am talking about Christ and the church. However, each one of you also must love his wife as he loves himself, and the wife must respect her husband. (vv. 31–33)

Certainly, this is a profound mystery.

The Marriage Ideal: Reciprocal Love and Respect

Paul takes us back to the culture of the Garden of Eden before sin, back to God's original plan for marriage. When we go back to marriage as God originally intended it, in Genesis 2:24 we read that the first couple became "one flesh." Genesis 2:24 is quoted four times in the New Testament. In Mark 10:7–8 and Matthew 19:5 Jesus quotes it to describe God's purpose for unity in marriage and to reason against divorce. In 1 Corinthians 6:16 Paul refers to it as a warning against sexual immorality, and in Ephesians 5:31 he uses it as a metaphor for the union of Christ and the church. God's original blueprint for marriage is void of shame and blame and is without rulership and subordination. Each partner thrives as both husband and wife honor and obey God; because both spouses honor and obey God, they also love, honor, and respect each other. Would not part of our Christian mission be to "reverse the curse" through Jesus' gift of redemption rather than to perpetuate the curse?

Whether we view Ephesians 5 as a description of mutuality or a prescription for hierarchy, the end result calls for a self-sacrificing love that puts another's interest over one's own. It calls for husbands to love their wives as their own selves and for wives to show their husbands respect.

How might this apply when a married couple has a conflict and arrives at an impasse? Hierarchists would conclude that the husband should make the final call. Others would conclude that husband and wife have equal say. While a couple may choose to function either way, I believe there is a better way to submit to one another in these types of discussions. When my husband and I get "stuck" between opinions, we ask each other how much the subject at hand matters to each of us. The one who feels less strongly about the issue under discussion will usually acquiesce to the one who has the stronger feelings about the issue. If we disagree with each other and both feel strongly about our view, we bring a trusted couple into our discussion. This is a great help. While this book is not a book on discipling relationships, I want to state that cultivating a trusted relationship with another couple (or two) who knows you well and helps you along the way is crucial to navigating difficult times and decisions in marriages.

You may ask, *So are you saying a wife does not need to submit to her husband?* Absolutely not. A wife has a high calling from Christ, as does her husband. A wife is called to submit to her husband. He may or may not be considerate. Equally difficult is the husband's call to lay down his life for his wife, loving her as Christ loves the church. This would be his high calling even if his wife is disrespectful and does not treat him well. Jesus set the example for us through his self-sacrifice and submission as demonstrated in scriptures such as 1 Peter 2:20–3:7. Only through Jesus' example and the power of his Spirit can we live in self-sacrifice to each other. Each person must be responsible for his/her own actions, whether it is easy or difficult.

Since Jesus submitted himself to death on a cross, does this mean a woman (or a man) should stay in an abusive marriage situation where their safety is at risk? The laws of the land where I live are strict on abuse, and thankfully, we are protected by those laws. I would advise any man or woman to seek safety in the shelter of these laws, which the Scriptures call us to obey. Unfortunately, women in many ancient hierarchal cultures did not have such options for seeking safety. Thus, the biblical teachings on how to treat one another were (and still are) much higher callings than the laws of the land.

I have heard many excellent lessons about love and respect taken from Ephesians 5. These lessons often teach that women need to feel loved and men need to feel respected. But as I have listened to these lessons I have felt that something was missing. I believe it is every bit as important for women to feel respected in order to feel loved, and for men to feel loved in order to feel respected. It goes both ways. *Simple tor / Reductionist thinking*

The relationship between a husband and wife serves either as a shining light or a stumbling block to the world around them. Since a wife's lack of submission could malign the word of God (Titus 2:5), we see that the marital dynamic can play a role in winning a husband's soul to Christ. Consider this: In a modern culture where a man may value his wife as an equal partner and the two may function in mutuality, an insistence that he and his wife embrace the traditional kind of patriarchal submission may actually hinder him from being won to Christ. As William J. Webb states, "By *actually* doing the text (literal imperative), we may no longer be doing the *intent* of the text (the purpose statement)."[84]

Thoughts to ponder.

I believe the heart behind these verses in Ephesians 5 is the most important focus. While we can learn the definition of complementarian and egalitarian, I think they can point us toward the wrong emphases. The "ian" I most prefer is Christ-ian. Christlike.

10

Embracing Paradoxes

The kingdom of God is full of paradoxes. Thoughts that make no sense apart from the cross of Christ: you must die to live; God offers both judgment and unconditional love; we have choice *and* we are bound by our sinful nature; we must give up our life to find our life. I believe we must embrace some paradoxes when we consider the role of husband and wife in marriage. I believe these paradoxes are also applicable when we discuss women's roles.

Michelle Lee-Barnewell expresses this concept in her book *Neither Complementarian nor Egalitarian:*

> Egalitarians can reconsider the role of authority and leadership, as these have often been downplayed in promoting mutual submission. Complementarians can reexamine what they mean by servant leadership. We have shown that "servant" is more than a modifier of "leadership" because in the kingdom both are present in a paradoxical relationship. Since Jesus and Paul claim authority even as they speak of being servants and slaves, an additional area of study may be how these two aspects are reconciled or otherwise coexist. The full impact of "reversal" must come into play, since the New Testament challenges hierarchy to show God's power, and the cross of Christ was the ultimate display of power working through weakness. The theme of "reversal" is critical for understanding how God's value system impacts believers in their relationship with God and others and in their self-understanding. In regard to leadership, servanthood does not simply qualify leadership but transforms it....
>
> What "authority," "leadership," "equality," and "rights" have in common is that they often highlight the individual over the community and God himself. What their reversals share is the potential to guide us to a greater acknowledgment of God's sovereignty and a recognition of God's ways in

which the willing sacrifice for the other through the denial of self-interest results in unity and love.[85]

While Jesus was given all authority, his life reflects the absolute submission of his own will in order to bring salvation to his beloved bride, the church. Make no mistake: We are called to account and there will be a judgment. While fear may be the beginning of wisdom, maturity does not respond out of fear of judgment (1 John 4:16-18). Because of Jesus' great love for us, we yield and submit to his will. Whenever we engage in battles for control, we all lose—and our relationships suffer. Thus, no matter what I personally believe about topics like the ones we are discussing in this book, my greater goal is to be a supportive, loving, and respectful ligament in the church.

In the church, leadership (usually a plurality of elders or a team of leaders including elders and others) has God-given authority to lead (Hebrews 13:17), to refute false teaching, and to discipline Christians who will not repent (Titus 1:9; Titus 2:15). Their authority is not to be based upon their opinions, whims, or desires, but upon the word of God. God protects his church in this way. His goal is not to empower individuals, but to build a community of believers who shine the light of Jesus on a dark world.

If Two Equals One in Marriage, Am I Complete or a Half?

Numerous women in our churches are single. Some are divorced; still others are widows. Others have husbands who are not Christians. Yet all women (and men) are complete when united with Christ. Completely complete.

I used to wonder how I would respond if I lost someone dear to me to illness or death. Now I face a very difficult prognosis with my husband's health. Every day I grieve Wyndham's suffering, even as somehow, God enables us to experience peace and joy beyond human understanding. I know that no matter which of us may leave this earth first, the one left behind will be indescribably sad, but will also be complete—with much still to give because we have Christ in us, the hope of glory.

Through my years of marriage, and yes, through Wyndham's illness, I have learned that if we depend on our spouse for our completion as a person, we are unable to give out of our fullness in

Christ—and our "giving spirit" becomes more dependent upon what we receive.

It is often difficult for a woman to believe she is complete in and of herself (with God). (The same thought can hold true for a man.) Many factors in our culture can influence a woman to believe that without a spouse, she is "less than." She often finds fewer clear opportunities in which she can fully use her gifts—and unfortunately, this is too often true in the church.

Women can buy into the famous words spoken in the movie *Jerry Maguire*: "You complete me." Though I understand this sentiment, I believe it is crucial that women (and men) be convinced that they are valuable as a complete person whether or not they are married. Even when married, if partnership is not valued between genders it can be easy to feel "less than."

We All Have Gifts to Give.

Since we were all created in the image of God, we are designed with specific and unique gifts and talents which are meant to be shared. When we don't use our talents and gifts, we feel unfulfilled and the body of Christ loses strength. As Paul explains in 1 Corinthians 12:12-31, this concept of using our gifts is applied to the communal body of Christ. The church, the body of Christ, has many parts that make up one body—just like the human body. Our baptism makes us (the body parts) equal, all sharing the same Spirit.

Paul goes on to describe the interdependence of the parts of the body and how the weaker parts are often some of the most important or necessary parts—contrary to what we might think. Each part has a function and no part is superior. Likewise, there are specific needed functions in the spiritual communal body, and each part has a gift to bring.

It is quite clear that men and women are different. Biology confirms this fact. Certainly in family roles, both father and mother have important and necessary roles to fulfill (1 Thessalonians 11-12; Ephesians 6:4; Hebrews 12:10; 1 Thessalonians 2:7; 2 Timothy 1:5). However, it can also be said that men and women have different gift sets among themselves. According to 1 Corinthians 12:12-27, these are meant to work together to make the body complete.

When we bring this example into family life, we must recognize that spouses' individual gift sets may or may not align with traditional roles. I can think of numerous examples where husbands have felt it was their leadership responsibility to manage the money and their wives' responsibility to manage the kitchen. In many cases, frustration resulted—along with disaster in the wallet and chaos in the kitchen—simply because cultural values ruled over giftedness.

A friend (a father and an evangelist) once shared an insight that resonated with me;

> I think our culture influences us to put value where God holds none. If culture were to value certain 'male' or 'female' attributes (if there, in fact, are such things) then we will be tempted to do the same. For me, it is difficult to step away from all this and hold a truly objective view. Those who claim they can are naively out of touch.

Another male friend once expressed his thoughts to me on why there must be a leader in a relationship or communal setting: "If three guys parachute into hostile territory, *someone has to be the leader or they will die.*" However, I asked my friend what he would think if two of the "guys" were men and one was a woman—and suppose the men did not have the gift of leadership and were hesitant to make decisions, but the woman was gifted with leadership talents. Should the woman wait for a man to lead? My friend replied, "Well I guess the woman had better open her mouth and start leading quickly."

We all have gifts to bring. Let us encourage others to use their gifts, never discouraging another from bringing their gift(s) to the table or competing about whose gift is more important. As another of Jesus' paradox states—it is in giving we receive.

> In everything I did, I showed you that by this kind of hard work we must help the weak, remembering the words the Lord Jesus himself said: 'It is more blessed to give than to receive.'" (Acts 20:35)

The "One-Another Way" Has No Gender Boundaries

Consider some of Paul's more general writings about how we are to treat one another regardless of gender. The "one another" scriptures apply equally to men and women. How radically transformed our relationships to one another would be if we applied these scriptures to *all* of our relationships *all* of the time.

> Be devoted to one another in love. Honor one another above yourselves. (Romans 12:10)

> Live in harmony with one another. Do not be proud, but be willing to associate with people of low position. Do not be conceited (Romans 12:16)

> Let no debt remain outstanding, except the continuing debt to love one another, for whoever loves others has fulfilled the law. (Romans 13:8)

> I myself am convinced, my brothers and sisters, that you yourselves are full of goodness, filled with knowledge and competent to instruct one another. (Romans 15:14)

> I appeal to you, brothers and sisters, in the name of our Lord Jesus Christ, that all of you agree with one another in what you say and that there be no divisions among you, but that you be perfectly united in mind and thought. (1 Corinthians 1:10)

> You, my brothers and sisters, were called to be free. But do not use your freedom to indulge the flesh; rather, serve one another humbly in love. (Galatians 5:13)

> Be completely humble and gentle; be patient, bearing with one another in love. (Ephesians 4:2)

> Be kind and compassionate to one another, forgiving each other, just as in Christ God forgave you. (Ephesians 4:32)

> Submit to one another out of reverence for Christ. (Ephesians 5:21)

> Bear with each other and forgive one another if any of you has a grievance against someone. Forgive as the Lord forgave you. (Colossians 3:13)

> Let the message of Christ dwell among you richly as you teach and admonish one another with all wisdom through psalms, hymns, and songs

from the Spirit, singing to God with gratitude in your hearts. (Colossians 3:16)

Therefore encourage one another and build each other up, just as in fact you are doing. (1 Thessalonians 5:11)

I have included these scriptures because I believe they are the relational target for which all Christians aim. Let us not become so focused on the "arrows" that we miss the target. When it comes to Ephesians 5, I wonder if we ask the wrong question. It's easy to focus on who is in charge, rather than how we should relate to one another.

Personal Reflection

As I began this study I came to realize that I have spent most of my life adopting a close semblance of the hierarchal complementarian view of gender roles in my marriage, and I have taught and written accordingly. Because I have a godly husband and we have practiced mutual love and respect in our marriage, we have experienced so much of the joy and fulfillment God intended for marriage. Our marriage has not been without struggle, but the struggles have resolved when we have committed to practice Jesus' way. Now, having more thoroughly studied these topics, I have found that the way my husband and I relate to one another and treat one another remains the same, although my viewpoint has shifted. I believe the Bible teaches "headship." I just think we often emphasize the wrong focus.

The question of whether or not Paul is calling wives to submit to their husbands in a hierarchal or non-hierarchal way in Ephesians 5 is not personally troubling to me—if I hold to the transcending principles of humility, consideration, and submission to Christ. I am called, as a disciple of Jesus (he who is the ultimate example of submission) to submit to my husband and to "one another." My husband, likewise, is called to submit to Christ *and* to one another. I think I can safely assume that I am included in "one another"—which means that because we are Christians, my husband and I will both submit to one another at times. We will each consider the other's needs before our own. We will sometimes give up our own desires so the other may thrive. Therein lies the protection and beauty of God's perfect plan! The "yin and the yang" of laying down our lives for one another as Jesus taught brings beautiful harmony, closeness, and intimacy.

As I write this book I am a servant to my husband in ways far beyond any of my previous experiences with him. I am not only comfortable with this new role, but I count serving him as an immense privilege and honor. Wyndham is ill with an aggressive and progressive neurological disease. I now do almost everything for him, from turning him over in bed, to dressing and meeting his hygiene needs, to preparing and feeding him all his food, to being his scribe, to helping him from his wheelchair to the bed and back again. I do this not because I am called to submit, but because I love him with an agape love. Truth be told, if our situations were switched, he would do the exact same things for me, loving me as Christ loves the church, laying down his life for me.

Jesus: The Ultimate Example of Submission

Let's take a step back from the discussion of submission in marriage to consider submission and humility in the life of Christ—and the Christian. It's tempting to get so focused on the marriage issue that we lose a sense of our overall goal as Christians: to become like our Lord, clothing ourselves with the kind of selfless humility he taught us. Jesus demonstrated how to submit—and love—as he sacrificed everything. In all our relationships—marriage, family, friendship, church family—we are meant to be like him. He who forgave rather than retaliated. He who, more than any of us, experienced "unfair." He who submitted to the will of his Father and to our need to be saved. He who ultimately laid down his life for us.

> Your attitude should be the same as that of Christ Jesus:
> Who, being in very nature God,
> did not consider equality with God something to be grasped,
> but made himself nothing,
> taking the very nature of a servant,
> being made in human likeness.
> And being found in appearance as a man,
> he humbled himself
> and became obedient to death—even death on a cross!
> (Philippians 2:5–8 NIV 1984)

As imperfect humans, we don't always practice these scriptures as well as we'd like, so what does this passage mean in practical terms for men and women today?

In Philippians 2, we understand that Jesus submitted to the will of his Father while he was on earth. While God and Jesus are completely one, Jesus—the Son of Man, the Word who was God and who dwelled among us—submitted to the Father while on earth. We have no reason to believe that God forced Jesus to go to earth and to give up his life for us. Jesus chose to do so because of his love for us, and God's love for us allowed it. Their relationship is an intimate intricacy of love and unity—one that is beyond our human understanding. A profound mystery.

Do We Really Want Fair?

While it can be tempting to think that any form of subordination is unfair, let's stop for a moment to consider: Do we really want "fair?" What do I (we) deserve? Honestly, what I deserve is to die and be eternally separated from God. Because of my sin, I am not entitled to the salvation I enjoy and hold as the most precious gift in my life. I don't deserve it. I wonder if we sometimes think God is lucky to have us. The call of Philippians 2, to empty ourselves, is difficult. It is hard to truly embrace and live by the truth that we don't deserve anything.

The way of the cross allows us to demonstrate a divine character in which we practice mutual submission. The way of the cross allows us to rise above retaliation when we aren't treated righteously or fairly. It is this Christlike attitude of submission to one another that radically changes our relationships. Jesus' words, as Luke recorded them, are not easy:

> "So watch yourselves. If your brother or sister sins against you, rebuke them, and if they repent, forgive them. Even if they sin against you seven times in a day, and seven times come back to you saying 'I repent,' you must forgive them."
>
> The apostles said to the Lord, "Increase our faith!"
>
> He replied, "If you have faith as small as a mustard seed, you can say to this mulberry tree, 'Be uprooted and planted in the sea,' and it will obey you.
>
> "Suppose one of you has a servant plowing or looking after the sheep. Will he say to the servant when he comes in from the field, 'Come along now

and sit down to eat'? Won't he rather say, 'Prepare my supper, get yourself ready and wait on me while I eat and drink; after that you may eat and drink'? Will he thank the servant because he did what he was told to do? So you also, when you have done everything you were told to do, should say, 'We are unworthy servants; we have only done our duty.' " (Luke 17:7–10)

These, my friends, are challenging scriptures. Although Jesus could have called legions of angels to take him off the cross and smite those who had put him there, he entrusted himself to him who judges justly, and then said, "Father forgive them; they don't know what they are doing." That's unfathomable love.

Although God could, as the ultimate authority, destroy us all at any moment, he gives us grace instead—almighty as he is, he humbles himself to raise us up:

> You give me your shield of victory,
>   and your right hand sustains me;
>   you stoop down to make me great. (Psalm 18:35 NIV 1984)

Jesus demonstrated this same humility as he laid down his life for all people— including his enemies.

Humility in Authority

[Yin + Tang / Balance]

God has established authority among people on earth to help us keep order among ourselves, but he also calls us to imitate his example of humility and love. In this we find another of God's amazing two-sided truths: God makes the rules, and he makes them for our good. God's intentions for authority stand in stark contrast to the world's power struggles and attitudes of entitlement.

Consider this example: While the Bible clearly teaches that elders hold responsibility and authority from God, Peter describes the elder's role in a paradoxical way:

> To the elders among you, I appeal as a fellow elder and a witness of Christ's sufferings and one who also will share in the glory to be revealed: Be shepherds of God's flock that is under your care, watching over them—not because you must, but because you are willing, as God wants you to be; not pursuing dishonest gain, but eager to serve; not lording it over those

entrusted to you, but being examples to the flock. And when the Chief Shepherd appears, you will receive the crown of glory that will never fade away.

In the same way, you who are younger, submit yourselves to your elders. All of you, clothe yourselves with humility toward one another, because,

> "God opposes the proud
> but shows favor to the humble." (1 Peter 5:1–5 NIV 2011)

Obedience was not a bad word to Jesus. In fact, obedience was something he learned through suffering (Hebrews 5:8) and a quality he practiced. He went first and set the example for us. Jesus recognized that we will all experience "unfairness" in relationships (just as he did), and he called us to have a righteous response. Jesus' example gives us the ultimate example of how to respond in a godly way to unfairness.

> To this you were called, because Christ suffered for you, leaving you an example, that you should follow in his steps.
> "He committed no sin,
> and no deceit was found in his mouth."
> When they hurled their insults at him, he did not retaliate; when he suffered, he made no threats. Instead, he entrusted himself to him who judges justly. "He himself bore our sins in his body" on the cross, so that we might die to sins and live for righteousness; "by his wounds you have been healed." For "you were like sheep going astray," but now you have returned to the Shepherd and Overseer of your souls. (1 Peter 2:21–25)

Living It Out

Jesus teaches us that godly leadership begins with personal example. We would do well to read and recommit our hearts to the following Scriptures often:

> Therefore I, a prisoner for serving the Lord, beg you to lead a life worthy of your calling, for you have been called by God. Always be humble and gentle. Be patient with each other, making allowance for each other's faults because of your love. Make every effort to keep yourselves united in the Spirit, binding yourselves together with peace. For there is one body and

one Spirit, just as you have been called to one glorious hope for the future. (Ephesians 4:1–4 NLT)

Is there any encouragement from belonging to Christ? Any comfort from his love? Any fellowship together in the Spirit? Are your hearts tender and compassionate? Then make me truly happy by agreeing wholeheartedly with each other, loving one another, and working together with one mind and purpose.

Don't be selfish; don't try to impress others. Be humble, thinking of others as better than yourselves. Don't look out only for your own interests, but take an interest in others, too.

You must have the same attitude that Christ Jesus had.
> Though he was God,
>> he did not think of equality with God
>> as something to cling to.
> Instead, he gave up his divine privileges;
>> he took the humble position of a slave
>> and was born as a human being.
> When he appeared in human form,
>> he humbled himself in obedience to God
>> and died a criminal's death on a cross.

(Philippians 2:1–8 NLT)

Here there is no Gentile or Jew, circumcised or uncircumcised, barbarian, Scythian, slave or free, but Christ is all, and is in all.

Therefore, as God's chosen people, holy and dearly loved, clothe yourselves with compassion, kindness, humility, gentleness and patience. (Colossians 3:11–12 NIV)

If I speak in the tongues of men and of angels, but have not love, I am only a resounding gong or a clanging cymbal. If I have the gift of prophecy and can fathom all mysteries and all knowledge, and if I have a faith that can move mountains, but have not love, I am nothing. If I give all I possess to the poor and surrender my body to the flames, but have not love, I gain nothing.

Love is patient, love is kind. It does not envy, it does not boast, it is not proud. It is not rude, it is not self-seeking, it is not easily angered, it keeps no record of wrongs. Love does not delight in evil but rejoices with the truth. It always protects, always trusts, always hopes, always perseveres. (1 Corinthians 13:1–7 NIV 1984)

The View from Paul's Window:

All these scriptures—and the principles they espouse—apply to both genders. When Christians practice these transcending principles, women respect men, and men respect women. Women will respect other women and men respect other men. Humility and submission to one another reign. Competition comes crashing down. Rudeness, anger, selfishness, and the desire to impress others go away, replaced by protection, trust, perseverance, grace, and the ability to work together with one mind and purpose. These qualities come from love and result in unity—the kind Paul describes in 1 Corinthians 13:4-7. The kind that Adam and Eve experienced before they sinned. The kind that Jesus longs for us to imitate in him.

These are transcending principles. If Christians were to truly follow these principles, there would be no need for the corrective scriptures. However, since we are not perfect, corrective principles will always apply in some way. If we truly take the Scriptures from the pages into our hearts and put them into practice in all our relationships, there will be no more self-focus, no favoritism, no prejudice, no bullying, no disrespect, no competition.

Our relationships—the way we value and treat one another—are where the church can shine the brightest in a "me-first" world. If Philippians 2—and its teachings on humbling ourselves, doing nothing out of selfish ambition, and giving up all our privileges—are truly our mantra, then the message of Jesus—and we his people—will "shine like stars in the universe as we hold out the word of life" (Philippians 2:15-16).

Truly, the only way we can do this is to practice the presence of Christ in us as we gain our identity and confidence from him. Only one who knows their true identity in God will be set free to give so unselfishly.

Men and women alike are called to be completely humble and gentle and to become like Jesus, emptying ourselves and putting others' good before our own.

As we embrace the paradoxes of Jesus, our relationships will be transformed and will stand in contrast against a self-focused world.

> "Whoever finds their life will lose it, and whoever loses their life for my sake will find it." (Matthew 10:39)

Women as Fellow Workers

Jesus viewed women as fellow workers, as did Paul.

Women were the first people Jesus commissioned to announce his resurrection. In his letter to the church in Rome (written around 56–57 AD), Paul describes women as fellow workers. It is significant that he does not refer to them as subordinates, but instead describes them with value, respect, and equality. I sometimes wonder if Paul, remembering with great remorse his former days as a persecutor of Christians, still heard in memory the cries of the devoted Christian women he had dragged off to prison. Paul's respect for his sisters shines as he affectionately describes his working relationship with devoted Christian women with whom he now shares the same heart and purpose.

Dear Friends and Fellow Workers

What a beautiful picture Paul paints as he describes men and women who are dear friends, fellow workers, and even fellow prisoners. Note the number of women in this list (their names are in bold):

> I commend to you our sister **Phoebe**, a servant of the church in Cenchrea.
> I ask you to receive her in the Lord in a way worthy of the saints and to give her any help she may need from you, for she has been a great help to many people, including me.
> Greet **Priscilla** and Aquila, my fellow workers in Christ Jesus. They risked their lives for me. Not only I but all the churches of the Gentiles are grateful to them.
> Greet also the church that meets at their house.

The View from Paul's Window:

Greet my dear friend Epenetus, who was the first convert to Christ in the province of Asia.

Greet **Mary**, who worked very hard for you.

Greet Andronicus and **Junias**, my relatives who have been in prison with me. They are outstanding among the apostles, and they were in Christ before I was.

Greet Ampliatus, whom I love in the Lord.

Greet Urbanus, our fellow worker in Christ, and my dear friend Stachys.

Greet Apelles, tested and approved in Christ.

Greet those who belong to the household of Aristobulus.

Greet Herodion, my relative.

Greet those in the household of Narcissus who are in the Lord.

Greet **Tryphena and Tryphosa**, those women who work hard in the Lord.

Greet my dear friend **Persis**, another woman who has worked very hard in the Lord.

Greet Rufus, chosen in the Lord, and **his mother**, who has been a mother to me, too.

Greet Asyncritus, Phlegon, Hermes, Patrobas, Hermas and the brothers with them.

Greet Philologus, **Julia**, Nereus and his **sister**, and Olympas and all the saints with them.

Greet one another with a holy kiss.

All the churches of Christ send greetings. (Romans 16:1–16 NIV 1984)

In a passage addressed to Euodia and Syntyche (Philippians 4:2–3), Paul describes how these two women had worked beside him, not under him. These two women had struggled alongside Paul, laboring with him; the Greek word he uses to describe their work denotes athletes working as a team, playing the game together as one person with one goal in mind. While Paul was a leader, the women who worked with him weren't at the bottom of a pyramid with Paul at the top; rather, they worked beside him on the playing field, the church. When Paul calls these women to agree with one another, he *appeals* to them—he doesn't use his "apostle card" and demand that they "fall in line."

Specific Roles for Women

In Acts 21:9, Philip's four daughters are said to prophesy. I have not heard many lessons on this subject, but it certainly seems the early church allowed women, like Philip's daughters, to hold a role in which they explained and expounded upon the scriptures.

Anna (Luke 2:36–38) was elderly, a widow, and a prophetess. She announces the infant Jesus' identity to those awaiting Israel's redemption. Is it possible that those who heard her were not simply temple visitors, but perhaps a group who had specific expectations about Jerusalem's redemption—a group led by Anna? Her title of prophetess suggests that she was surrounded in some way by people who viewed her teaching as authoritative. She would have had many opportunities to prophesy, since the passage tells us she never left the temple.

Did women like Philip's daughters prophesy to the whole church, or specifically to the women—or does God leave the description in scripture ambiguous for a reason? We may never know. However, we can learn much from Paul's list of women in the ministry in Romans 16. In Romans 16, Phoebe is recognized as a servant, and it seems she held a specific role within the church.[86] Romans 16 includes the names of women who seemed to be leaders within their house churches. Did they preach and teach in these settings? We know they prophesied and prayed, so in some form it certainly appears they did.

Women with the gifts of leadership are not only needed to minister to women, but they are also needed to advise other leaders, to serve on leadership teams and boards, and as their gift set applies, to chair boards and committees.

In our culture today, the Internet is a powerful tool for teaching and preaching. This past weekend I listened to a lesson on YouTube, taught by a woman to a women's midweek. Inspired by her powerful words, I recommended and sent the link to several men and women who were eager to listen to it—they all found it helpful, men and women alike. Is this not a form of preaching? My question is, does the size of the audience cause a woman's lesson to usurp authority—in other words, is it okay for her to speak to a small group but not a large one? If the size of the audience matters, what is the deciding number? (And what do we do about the limitless possibilities of the

Internet audience?)

Does the issue of women usurping men's authority (1 Timothy 2) restrict women from teaching the scriptures in a mixed audience? Or was the restriction culturally and situationally specific (again, because the new women were usurping authority and most likely questioning Paul's authority as an apostle)? Questions to ponder.

Thoughts on Church Life

While I began my study simply seeking to understand the difficult scriptures Paul taught about women, life brought me more questions. During my study I received unsolicited questions about why we did not have discussions on these matters in the church. And the inquiries weren't just from women. Men and women are reading books like the ones I have referenced and are also unsure how to answer their friends and neighbors who ask them about the role of women in the church. I looked for a book on this topic from someone from my own church background, but I could find no such book. So, in the words of Toni Morrison, the 1993 Nobel Prize winner in Literature, "If there's a book that you want to read, but it hasn't been written yet, then you must write it."

Regardless of your view on where and when women may teach the scriptures, it seems clear that churches are greatly benefited when women's influence is sought and included. In years past, many churches have restricted women's participation and influence to duties and roles that their culture defined as "women's tasks"—things like childcare, food planning, decorating, and the counseling of other women. But women's influence is valuable and needed in making important decisions for churches! I have seen firsthand the wisdom, effectiveness, and beauty of teams of men and women working together to discuss the needs and direction of churches. Both the male and female viewpoint have added to the discussion and perspective.

But this only works when the men and women—all the people in the room and on the team—put on the character of Christ: complete humility and gentleness, counting others as better than themselves. If anyone, male or female, does not conduct themselves with a spirit of humility, selflessness, and submission, the chemistry of meetings or gatherings becomes competitive and volatile rather than peaceful and constructive.

Paul's Teachings on Women

And what about women speaking in public assemblies? Of course, that decision must be decided by the leadership of each church. I believe the church will be far more effective in reaching the lost world (and strengthening the saved) when we hear from both men and women in our services. The opportunity to hear from each other's focus on Jesus and the ways he has changed our lives can serve as a true unity booster and can reach hearts in unique ways.

I am grateful for what I experience in worship services in my local church. The congregation is usually welcomed by a man and a woman, a communion message is given by a man and a woman (usually with the majority of the allotted time given to the woman), men and women serve as ushers, baptisms of women are administered by sisters, and the sermon may have a section in which a sister participates. I don't believe the services are designed this way simply to keep the women happy and give the appearance of gender equality, but because meaningful participation by women better meets the church's needs and is in keeping with the scriptures.

Specific Questions

Can a woman teach a mixed audience? It certainly seems this would be dependent upon her attitude. If she berated a group or took over while someone else was leading, she would be acting inappropriately. But if she exhibits an attitude of humility I see no reason from the scriptures to exclude her. The church benefits from the experiences and perspectives of both men and women teaching and speaking. Again, while this is practiced in many churches in various ways, conversations about such practices must unfold with appropriate respect and patience.

Can a woman perform a wedding? Certainly that depends upon the laws of the land. If a woman is permitted by her local government to do so, I find nothing in the scriptures that states otherwise. Whatever our views on biblical authority in the church, the state gives the authority to "legally wed" a couple.

The subject of women's role in the church is a hot topic for many. Wisdom must dictate how we implement what is permissible within the context of what is best for all. Sometimes the scriptures may permit things that are not best in a particular situation at a certain time. As Paul puts it,

"I have the right to do anything," you say—but not everything is beneficial. "I have the right to do anything"—but not everything is constructive. No one should seek their own good, but the good of others. (1 Corinthians 10:23–24 NIV)

> Let us be careful not to "push the envelope" simply to prove a point. We must, like Paul, aim for God's transcending principles while carefully maintaining an awareness and respect for our current cultural views in ways that promote unity. Promoting agendas or "proving points" does not promote unity. Not ever. Laying aside our rights for the good of a whole is always best. And that means we may have to be patient if our particular congregation is not ready for as much change as scripture may allow.

Invited to the Table

I am always moved when I picture the emotional scene of joyful, amazed disciples standing on the Mount of Olives staring at the sky after Jesus' resurrection and ascension (Acts 1). I can barely imagine this scene, but I am sure it was indelibly stamped in the minds of those who experienced it.

Can you imagine what you would have felt if Jesus had left his mission to the world with *you*? (Spoiler alert: He did!) Jesus had lived beside and loved his team of disciples, which we know included both men and women. How I would love to have heard the conversations (or lack thereof) among the disciples during the half-mile walk back to Jerusalem after the ascension. When they arrived in Jerusalem they all went to the upper room to pray (Acts 1:12–14). There was no outer chamber or separate place for the women in the upper room—men and women, they were all together in their love for Jesus and their zeal for his mission. They must have wondered what they should do next—perhaps they dreamed and strategized together. It's significant to note that their plans for "what to do next" began with days of prayer together. They would take their cues from God's Spirit guiding their lives. Simple but profound, a practice we would do well to imitate.

It seems natural to assume that the men and women prayed together in the upper room, as the women were disciples too. They had been involved with Jesus in his ministry, and had at times led the way in their faith. In a counterculturual move, Jesus had invited women into his ministry. Among the apostles, the leaders who would spread the good news of Jesus around the world, Jesus made a seat at the table for the women—we have no reason to believe they were apostles, but they worked and prayed and served side by side among them.

What Might This Mean for Our Church?

I am deeply grateful for the strong and loving men who lead in our churches. In a world where many male leaders have failed in character and example, the church today shines brightly with men who love God wholeheartedly and value spirituality.

I believe my fellowship of churches has come a long way in seating women at the table, but perhaps we can grow by extending the welcome more heartily. This plea, of course, is more applicable to the men who already have a seat at the table. This welcome might begin with initiation—making a heartfelt effort to notice women's gifts and to seek their meaningful involvement and input. Inviting women to have a seat *with them* at the leadership table. (See Appendix C for an "out of the box" example.) I hope men who lead will welcome women's influence and wisdom as we work together on all sorts of issues facing the church. Women and men alike feel devalued when they can't find a place in the church to practice their God-given gifts. Jesus expects us to use our gifts (see the parable of the talents in Matthew 25). Burying our gifts is not pleasing to God. In fact, the master in the parable calls the one who does not use his/her allotted talent(s) wicked, lazy, and worthless. Yikes!

Some women (like some men) are gifted with leadership talents. Leadership is no more important than other gifts, but like other gifts, it must not be squashed. How sad it would be if cultural inhibitions and practices—practices that are not imposed by scripture—buried the gifts of people who are eager to use them. Let us not bury our gifts or be guilty of burying others' gifts. If women (or men) are not able to use their leadership gifts in the church (where they can help change people's eternal destinies), they will use them only in their careers or in much less meaningful ventures. Let us not contribute to such a tragedy.

Would we be willing for a woman to teach from her expertise and gift set, or would we rather choose a man to teach (a man who perhaps has less expertise in the area) simply because of his gender? If so, it may be helpful to reflect on the "why" and to consider the teachings we have explored in this book, if questions about women speaking are at the root of our hesitancy. At times women have wished to have Bible discussions in their workplace or university or school, but wonder if they can lead those discussions if a male leader can't be present.

Women desire to be valued for our contributions, for what we bring to the table—not because brothers feel obligated to "practice inclusiveness," but because our input and collaboration are desired, valued, and needed. They have much to contribute as presenters, teachers, worship team leaders, think tank participants, or strategy builders and have much needed insight to offer in these arenas.

Women want (and need) to be respected and consulted for their gifts of leadership, administration, teaching, and so on. Women don't want to be an afterthought when it comes to serving and contributing in the areas in which God has gifted them! Numerous topics of expertise are housed in the hearts and minds of women.

More than half the church is made up of women—women from all walks of life. Single women and women whose husbands do not serve in leadership can all too often be "invisible voices" or "hidden figures" within the church. It is good to remember that both Anna and Philip's prophesying daughters were single, and some of the widows in Corinth apparently had "official" roles in the church.

As I was writing this book, my personal situation changed, as I previously mentioned. Although I have served with my husband in the ministry for more than forty years, he became ill and can no longer work. I am fortunate because I remain employed as a minister and have plenty of work to do. However, I have known a number of women who desire to serve in the ministry, but whose jobs are dependent on their husband's employment in the ministry. Outside of ministry, capable women whose husbands do not serve in leadership (for various reasons) would be greatly encouraged to discover more ways within the church to use their gifts. These are not easy discussions, and solutions are not always clear, but I believe, with prayer and discussion, we can make progress.

Going Forward with Discernment

First, an appeal to women:

Sisters, for our part, if we are to come to the table we must be willing and eager to step up with the heart and mindset to fully engage. Also, if we come to the table primarily because we feel we deserve to be there, we won't come with a spirit of humility. Entitlement is not the way of the cross.

And thoughts for all of us: Communication is key. I remember a time early in our marriage when I cried and told Wyndham I felt like I was in a box and he needed to let me out of that box. We had both been raised in the same cultural setting that restricted the role of women in life, in church, and in marriage, and although I was eager to be my husband's greatest supporter I also knew I wanted to make a difference in this world and needed to be freed from my invisible box. My wonderful husband listened. Although it took time, prayer, struggle, and growth on both our parts, Wyndham became my greatest supporter, urging me to use my strengths and gifts from God. We became each other's biggest cheerleaders, and we have both been able to use our God-given gifts more fully in God's service ever since. I am eternally grateful for Wyndham's love and support for me (and for what I have written in this book). I believe and know he feels respected and loved, as do I.

This book is not about arguing for diversity or inclusiveness as a fellowship but rather about encouraging us to more fully hold to God's design for the church. Inspiring us to "fan into flame" the gifts and fruits of the Holy Spirit for all our members, male and female alike (2 Timothy 1:6; Galatians 5:22–23). Encouraging us all to work together to share in Paul's purpose of advancing the kingdom of God.

Let us look for ways to grow, despite our cultural predispositions and even our prejudices, to help each other use our God-given gifts to the full.

Today our mission should be the same as Paul's: to win as many as possible and to let the message of Christ shine in our world.

Perhaps by expanding some practices in our churches (within the confines of scripture, of course) we might win more people—both women and men—for Christ. Our twenty-first century Western culture holds dramatically different views on women's roles and gender relations than the first-century Jewish and Greco-Roman views—and it's not just that. The truth is, our church culture began to develop in the mid- to late-1900s, and since that time the role of American women has changed and expanded dramatically. Modern culture views women differently, and modern women view themselves differently. Young women in particular often wonder if the glass ceiling they perceive in our churches will allow them to fully contribute their gifts. While our current culture in no way changes the message of the Bible, I pray that our ongoing Bible study and conversations will result in our finding effective ways to follow Paul's trajectory (based on Jesus' teachings) toward the culturally transcendent targets of love, respect, and humility. In the pages of this book, I pray we have seen that God puts no ceilings on the beautiful, transcultural fruits of his nature.

> But the Holy Spirit produces this kind of fruit in our lives: love, joy, peace, patience, kindness, goodness, faithfulness, gentleness, and self-control. There is no law against these things!
>
> Those who belong to Christ Jesus have nailed the passions and desires of their sinful nature to his cross and crucified them there. Since we are living by the Spirit, let us follow the Spirit's leading in every part of our lives. Let us not become conceited, or provoke one another, or be jealous of one another. (Galatians 5:22–26 NLT)

Personal Reflection

As I shared in the introduction, many years ago I changed my theology about beer-drinking. I had no personal motive when I began my study about alcohol. I didn't change because I wanted to drink—it turns out I don't even like beer (except Bud Light Lime, which my husband assures me barely qualifies as beer at all). As I have said, I have not approached my study of women's roles with any axes to grind. I have plenty to do, I feel fulfilled in my Christianity, and I love being a married woman. I began this study simply because I wanted to know what the scriptures taught. As the Bible once surprised me by altering my thoughts about alcohol, so this study has adjusted my understanding of many of the scriptures about women—I believe my perspective is now more in line with what the scriptures teach, but I am still learning every day.

I believe the scriptures fully equip us to function in a variety of cultural settings—whether our culture looks more like Paul's (in which marriages functioned as a hierarchal pyramid and society was firmly patriarchal) or whether they look more like a level playing field. In both settings (and in countless nuanced variations in between), the scriptures apply and make us better, because the scriptures always aim for the heart—imitating the heart of Jesus who laid down his life for us.

I believe we must use wisdom in "where we go from here." When I was convinced from the scriptures that drinking beer was not sinful, I didn't respond by inviting the church over for a keg party or by making up for "the beers I never drank." Likewise, I do not plan to ask my preacher if I can preach the next time he goes out of town, nor do I want to. I did (do) not want to teach (or write) on such a complex topic without seeking wisdom and counsel. When we approach topics where differing opinions abound, they can become hot topics that divide, or valuable discussions leading to greater unity. Like Paul, we must be wise about threading the cultural settings in which we live and worship, and yet we need not apologize for what we believe the scriptures teach. This takes wisdom, time, and patience.

In *The Blue Parakeet: Rethinking How You Read the Bible,* Scot McKnight wrote,

> For Christians in Asian or Muslim cultural contexts, extending roles to what Scripture allows too fast could endanger the church's witness or credibility. But in much of the Western world, too little too slow could neutralize the church's impact in society just as effectively. What we need is discernment.[87]

Any time we approach change or challenges in the church, we must face and address the fears of leaders and members alike. Ultimately, we must revere God and his word. Changes must stem from careful teaching and instruction with gentleness and humility—not from a desire to do battle and "win." We must hold to the same passion as Paul—to see as many as possible make it to heaven.

> Even though I am a free man with no master, I have become a slave to all people to bring many to Christ. When I was with the Jews, I lived like a Jew to bring the Jews to Christ. When I was with those who follow the Jewish law, I too lived under that law. Even though I am not subject to the law, I did this so I could bring to Christ those who are under the law. When I am with the Gentiles who do not follow the Jewish law, I too live apart from that law so I can bring them to Christ. But I do not ignore the law of God; I obey the law of Christ.
>
> When I am with those who are weak, I share their weakness, for I want to bring the weak to Christ. Yes, I try to find common ground with everyone, doing everything I can to save some. I do everything to spread the Good News and share in its blessings. (1 Corinthians 9:19–23 NLT)

Back to Our Hermeneutic

Let us revisit the four principles we established in chapter one about interpreting scripture and applying it to women in the church.

1. The cultural expectations for a first-century woman's role were very different from the current Western expectations, so we need to read biblical passages considering those differences.
2. The New Testament explicitly states that men and women are equal, and yet some passages also seem to tacitly condone restrictions and hierarchy (between genders in general and in the marriage relationship), but those passages must be read and understood in light of the larger principles of the gospel.
3. Paul was carefully but consistently moving the believing communities in a new direction. He addressed them where they were, making allowances for their current culture, but he also consistently pointed them somewhere new. He tried to help his contemporaries to understand the implications of where the kingdom of God was taking them.
4. If we read past the cultural conditions that Paul had to deal with, and if we correctly apply the larger principles of the new covenant to our culture today, we may conclude that many of the restrictions Paul gave to women in the New Testament are no longer applicable.

I love the way author Ruth Barton expresses this:

> Women like Miriam, Huldah, Abigail, Esther, and Deborah demonstrated that "you can't keep a good woman down." When a woman was the right person for the job, whether it was leading in worship, prophesying, exhorting, saving a nation from genocide, or leading soldiers into battle, God didn't hesitate to use her. And the results were impressive.[88]

As we use our own gifts, and encourage each other to use theirs, may the world see our love for one another, and thus see Jesus more clearly. Let our practices reflect the transcending principles of God's nature so that Christ can be seen in us, and so that more and more will come to know him. May we focus less on the arrows and rather seek the target of Paul's admonition: "But the aim of such instruction is love that comes from a pure heart, a good conscience, and sincere faith" (1 Timothy 1:5 NRSV).

Appendix A

Author's note: This information was gathered primarily from research done by Brian J. Dodd in his book, *The Problem with Paul,* (InterVarsity Press, 1996), particularly a dissertation by S. Scott Bartchy.

American Chattel Slavery as Compared to Ancient Greco-Roman Slavery

Pre-Civil War slavery in the United States is considered "chattel slavery," and chattel slavery is the kind of enslavement most modern Westerners envision when they hear the word "slavery." Rightly, they envision a detestable practice with no redeeming qualities. As we will see, pre-Civil War chattel slavery in the U.S. had significant differences from the kind of slavery that existed when the New Testament was written (ancient Greco-Roman slavery)—the kind of slavery that Paul wrote about. The most important difference between the two is probably the first in the list below:

1. Chattel slavery–*Chattel* means a property or personal possession. In chattel slavery, a slave was owned for life as the owner's personal property. The slave's children and grandchildren would be automatically enslaved at birth.

    Greco-Roman slaves had hope of emancipation, often ten to twenty years after reaching adulthood. However, if a slave was a criminal, it was unlikely he or she would be freed.

2. Chattel slavery was abusive, degrading, and dehumanizing, with no opportunities for a better life.

    Greco-Roman slavery often brought opportunities for a better life. Some men and women sold themselves into slavery in hopes of advancement. Some slaves (usually in the cities) held high positions in businesses and in civil service. They served their masters as doctors, nurses, teachers, and companions (for example, as companions to elderly owners). They held business jobs as accountants, secretaries, sea captains, and officers of the court. Some were writers for their owners. However, some slaves in rural areas (particularly those who mined, farmed, or were prostituted) were treated abusively, similar to the way African slaves in the Southern United States were treated.

3. Chattel slavery was racial. White masters had African slaves transported from across the ocean.

   In ancient Greco-Roman slavery, slaves hailed from many different cultures and races, and were indistinguishable from the free.

4. Chattel slaves could not be educated. It was against the law to educate slaves. Greco-Roman slaves were often educated. Some served as tutors and were highly educated.

5. Chattel slaves were socially segregated, occupying the bottom of the social ladder. An ancient Greco-Roman slave would not stand out from anyone else. They were not easily distinguished by their occupation, their friends, or their worship.

6. Chattel slaves had no legal rights. Their treatment fell to the whims of their masters. Ancient Greco-Roman slaves had legal rights, including the right to appeal to higher authorities if they were treated unfairly.

7. Chattel slaves had no family life. Husbands, wives, and children were split up when they were sold. Ancient Greco-Roman slaves often had a separate family life, at times working another job to increase their savings.

8. Chattel slaves were kidnapped and sold. This slavery had no redeeming qualities and was a detestable practice.

   Although this was not always the case, ancient Greco-Roman slavery was seen (and chosen) by some slaves as a preferred way of life.[89]

Appendix B

Historical Highlights and Lowlights of Women: From Paul's Day Through the Restoration Movement

What was life like for women in the church in Paul's day? What happened "behind the curtain," where Paul could not see from his window? What happened in private homes? Did women enjoy the life they were created to live back in the garden? Hardly. Satan has continued to steer the world down his dark path, often dragging the church with it—though in contrast, many bright lights reflecting the image of Jesus continue to shine in the darkness, and the darkness cannot snuff them out.

If you have ever visited one of Walt Disney's theme parks, you may have experienced a popular ride called It's a Small World. Animated vignettes of life and culture across the globe are showcased as you ride around the world. A song by the same name plays throughout the ride—a song that is the ultimate earworm. Now that I have written this, I (and you) will likely be singing the song throughout the day: "It's a small world after all, it's a small, small world."

In this chapter, I will attempt to take you on a fast ride through approximately two thousand years of history, touching on some major historical events that affected the lives of women in the Western world. Buckle up! Unfortunately, during many sections of this historical ride (though not all), the accompanying song could easily be, "It's a man's world after all."

The First Century to the Dark Ages for Women

As we begin in the first century, where Paul left off, we speed through the Greco-Roman Empire, which showcases patriarchal influences from Aristotle's proclamations about the inferiority of women to Plato's degrading comments. The influence of Gnosticism in society and the church led many people to think that women were the body and men were the mind. Sexuality took center stage, and in reaction, asceticism grew more prevalent in Christian thought. In the fourth century, Augustine had a huge impact on the church as he espoused that men were rational and women irrational. He also asserted that sexuality weakened man, and since women could cause men sexual temptation, women should be kept out of sight.

Many church fathers felt that women (as descendants of Eve) were responsible for sin entering in the world, so (again) women must be kept out of sight lest man be tempted. This led to further segregation and subordination. Tertullian worked to organize Christianity as a legal entity. This led to basilicas (church buildings) replacing the house churches in which Christians had always met. Remaining celibate became the way to honor God, leading the way to monasteries and convents.

As we twist and turn on this ride, it gets darker as we approach the Medieval period (roughly 500–1000 AD). The fall of Rome ushered in the Dark Ages. In this time, historians tell us that ideas about women reached two extremes. On the one hand, women were painted as evil and inferior, while on the other hand, they were lauded as models of virtue and holiness. The doctrine of Mary as the idealized virgin stood in contrast to the image of woman as the witch, an idea that led to the horrific hatred of women during the witch craze that swept Europe between the fifteenth and sixteenth centuries.[90]

Many medieval theologians mirrored the writings of the earlier Greek philosophers (many of whom had also influenced the early church fathers). During the thirteenth century Thomas Aquinas espoused the same claim as Aristotle: women were created as subordinate and inferior to men with less intellectual ability and less ability to make correct moral decisions. Aquinas added that women were defective humans, a result of an accidental change to the male sperm, which under normal circumstances would always produce another male.[91]

Many women, desiring to serve God, found refuge in convents. Since monasteries were often located outside of the city wall they were more susceptible to pillaging and rape from barbaric bands of men. However, in the monasteries the nuns could escape arranged marriages and educate themselves. Some of the nuns rose to positions of privilege equal to those of bishops and noblemen because of their personal piety and shrewd management of convents.[92]

The Reformation and Women

By the sixteenth-century Reformation, the monasteries became known for their wealth and elegant lifestyle: "The worldly power of prince-bishops and the profligacy of the begging monks overshadowed the genuine spirituality that had birthed the (monastic) movement" a thousand years earlier.[93] So reformers began shutting down monasteries.

The church became politicized and corrupt. To fund the church-building boom and the Crusades, the church sold indulgences.

The ride gets a little brighter in the early 1500s as Martin Luther, in opposition to the corruption he saw in the church, nailed his 95 theses to the door of the principal church of Wittenberg for purposes of academic discussion, having no idea what scope of reformation his words would ignite. Reformation removed the stigma women had lived under for centuries, but culture still retained a patriarchal structure. Eve's sin still made women's role subordinate. Luther was clear that when his wife had taken his name and moved into his geographical space, she had acknowledged her subordination to him. However, reformers demanded universal education, which opened the door for many women to learn.

Our ride now turns a corner, where we see philosophers, artists, architects, and musicians. If we look closely we will see someone operating a moveable-type printing press.

The Renaissance

The Renaissance was made possible by several primary events. One was a migration of Greek scholars and texts to Italy—the influence of scholars had been lost to the West during the Middle Ages. Another was the invention of the printing press, which made it possible to disperse information. While one might assume the Renaissance would open more doors for women, the forward changes for women were mainly restricted to upper-class women, primarily in Italy.

The Renaissance and the Age of Enlightenment brought more independent thinking—these were precursors to the American Constitution and Declaration of Independence. However, a number of major Enlightenment thinkers still defaulted to patriarchal tradition for women.

The Enlightenment

Jean-Jacques Rousseau, an eighteenth-century philosopher whose thoughts and writings helped shape the Enlightenment, the French Revolution, and the development of political and educational thought, concluded that "women's entire education should be planned in relation to men. To please men, to be useful to them, to win their love and respect…these are women's duties in all ages and these are what they should be taught from childhood on."[94]

The Enlightenment gave birth to unintended anti-establishment revolutions, including the Industrial Revolution, political revolution (overturning the rule of monarchy in France and the US), and a religious revolution with evangelical revitalization. Immanuel Kant, a German philosopher credited as a central figure in modern philosophy, insisted that a husband has a "right to possess [his wife]…[and] a wife's duty to obey her husband is a demand of natural law as well as moral obligation."[95]

However, not all Enlightenment thinkers agreed, although Kant's views carried the day. The Marquis de Condorcet (a French philosopher of the Enlightenment) wrote a tract advocating women's full entrance into the public sphere, including the right to vote and hold public office.[96]

While one of the Enlightenment's core tenets was a person's right to "life, liberty, and the pursuit of happiness" (promoted by thinkers Locke and Hobbes), unfortunately this practically applied primarily to men of a certain class.

The Great Awakening

Our ride takes another turn in which we view religious revolution in the American colonies, beginning with the Great Awakening. This brought on greater divisions within religious groups. In 1800, only six percent of Americans were members of any kind of religious establishment, and most of those members were women.[97] By the end of the 1800s, women outnumbered male church members by a ratio of three to two. Alice Mathews notes that the country was first settled by those in pursuit of religious freedom who now lived with a freedom *from* religion.[98] To help fund struggling churches that no longer received state funding, it became necessary for ministers to change their views and cater more to women. They joined forces with women to try to bring men back to God.

Changes from the Industrial Revolution

Our ride's scenery changes dramatically as we enter the Industrial Revolution in America. Until now, families had worked together for survival. Business had always been conducted primarily from the home. Colonial wives knew the family business and could run it if something happened to their husbands. Children, particularly sons, served as apprentices to their fathers. But as we enter the Industrial Age, fathers migrated to the cities in pursuit of increased economic opportunities. As women were no longer part of their husband's external world and also had more money, many women had the opportunity to employ servants to perform domestic duties. The "pretty gentlewoman" emerged.

With moves to industrial towns and the ability to buy mass-produced goods, fathers would be absent from home for twelve to fourteen hours a day, six days a week. Parenting responsibilities fell on the mothers. Sons no longer worked with their dads, learning their skills. Mill owners could trap families by providing mandatory rental units for housing and factory stores in which families bought their goods. The stores were often located next to brothels or bars. Young children could work in the mills, and ties to the family weakened. Work life was now separated from home life.

At the close of the eighteenth century, the door opened for women's education with the formation of the earliest academies for girls and women. The language about women had changed from the witch, the whore, and the evil temptress to the "angel in the home."[99]

The Doctrine of Separate Spheres

Next on our ride we encounter a vignette of spheres, knows as the Doctrine of Separate Spheres.

Before we approached the Industrial Revolution portion of our ride, men could be seen doing work requiring physical strength, skill, and even physical risk. The patriarchal family structure supported a traditional masculine identity. A man's primary role was as a father, and sons were controlled through promised economic security passed down from the father.[98] But this changed in the Industrial

Revolution. Now men worked more sedentary jobs away from home. Historian Barbara Berg notes that men, now working at desks or machines and no longer doing work that encouraged or allowed them to develop the traditional (physical) manly identifiers, began insisting that women possessed all the weak and inferior traits. In order to maintain a "manly" view of themselves, men tended to further subjugate women, assigning inferior abilities to them.[100]

Thus, the Industrial Revolution gave rise to the doctrine of separate spheres, a new philosophy of womanhood. The press and clergy joined hands to separate women's spheres from men's spheres. Printed sermons, pamphlets, and newspaper articles taught about the dangers to women if they entered the man's sphere. Some physicians espoused that any woman who spent time using her mind would cause her reproductive organs to shrivel up and die. Her sphere was the home, and her role was glorified as the "angel of the home." Home was a man's castle and a woman's domain. In place by 1835, the Cult of True Womanhood (this was a philosophy that womanly virtue resided in piety, purity, submissiveness, and domesticity) arose from the doctrine of separate spheres. The True Woman, being free from the distractions faced by her husband in his work in the capitalistic democracy, was to be the moral guardian of the family, responsible for the comfort of the home and the spiritual formation of every family member. Historian Barbara Welter identified the True Woman with the four markers previously mentioned: piety, purity, submissiveness, and domesticity.[101]

With their new right to expand morality and religion across America, the True Women formed missionary societies, distributed Bibles, started Sunday schools to teach poor children religion and reading, and helped churches in poor sections of major cities. They paid preachers to minister to sailors and helped young men go through seminary. Their associations cared for orphans, widows, and indigent women. Some of these women went to brothels to pray and talk with prostitutes, hoping to lead them out of their godless professions; they also publicly listed the names of respected men who frequented these brothels.

As women used their gifts to create needed change, they also learned through their experiences how to run effective organizations. They became more confident and gained a sense of camaraderie and solidarity from their work and growth together. Clergy applauded their efforts, as long as they remained in the proper hierarchy. However, their unity and new skills brought on resistance to all kids of oppression directed again women. As women felt the need for more education, they began their own colleges in the late 1800s (Vassar, Smith, Wellesley, Radcliffe).

As we view this part of our ride through history, I am reminded of God's *ezer* and the idea that men and women were not meant to be alone. Men and women were meant to be fellow workers. In accordance with God's plan, women did not do all this work and forge all this change alone. They worked side by side with men as fellow workers.

The Victorian Era

As we view the next vignette of the Victorian era, extending from the mid-1800s to 1901, marriage had shifted from a partnership in which both husband and wife made meaningful contributions, to a relationship in which the husband produced all the income and the wife spent the income. This resulted in animosity and dissatisfaction, leaving many troubled and dissolved marriages in its wake.

The Restoration Movement and Women

This little journey brings us to a religious movement called the Restoration Movement (late 1700s to early 1900s; it is also known as the Stone-Campbell Movement). Denominations were many and traditions abounded; people longed to just "get back to the Bible" for direction. The desire of the Restoration Movement was not simply to reform a church gone astray from the will of God, but to restore unity and restore the church as it was meant to be when it was formed in the first century. My fellowship of churches has its roots in the Restoration Movement.

Members of the Restoration Movement embraced the opportunity to restore unity, slough off more than a thousand years of church tradition, and "go back to the beginning" of the church, back to the way it had been under the apostles' leadership. The Churches of Christ, the Christian Church, and the Disciples of Christ all have roots in the Restoration Movement, and from 1832–1906 they were among the fastest growing churches in America.

So how did the Restoration Movement view women? This is especially important for us to understand, as their views (on women and many other topics) have heavily influenced our church culture through the years.

In its infancy, the Restoration Movement offered many opportunities for women to lead (and to serve—let us remember that biblical leadership is servant leadership). In the 1800s the early Restoration writers assumed that the early church had a role for women known as the deaconess.

The phenomenon of women preachers was fairly common in the early Restoration Movement, especially in the eastern United States. In the Churches of Christ associated with Barton Stone (Stone was another key Restoration Movement leader), women preached, exhorted, and testified. One noted example was Nancy Mulkey, the daughter of a Separate Baptist preacher who led his congregation out of its denomination and into the Stone Movement in the early 1800s. Nancy served as an "exhorter" in the church.

Isaac Jones wrote, "[Nancy Mulkey] would arise with zeal in her countenance and fire in her eyes, and with a pathos that showed in the depths of her soul, and would pour forth an exhortation lasting from five to fifteen minutes, which neither father nor brother could equal, and which brought tears from every feeling eye."[102]

In 1845 Alexander Campbell (one of the main leaders of the Restoration Movement) wrote, "The primitive church had deacons. Such was Phoebe of Cenchrea. I say it [the church] is an organized body. Its organs are pastors, deacons, and deaconesses; and for foreign missions and influence, evangelists or missionaries." Campbell also wrote, "It is generally regarded, among our brethren, as an essential element in the restoration of the primitive order, to ordain, in every church, both deacons and deaconesses."[103]

However, as time went on, Campbell changed his views to match the culture of his day—in his culture, women were seen as belonging in the home (remember the Spheres). By the early 1900s, the Stone-Campbell Restoration Movement had relegated the woman's role to the home. Of note are several women who stood out not only in their homes, but also in their leadership in the church.

In the late 1800s and early 1900s, Clara Babcock was the Restoration Movement's first ordained female gospel preacher. A married woman and the mother to six children, Babcock actively engaged in preaching and teaching, eager to see many people find salvation in Christ. In an online article about Babcock's life and ministry, Bobby Valentine writes, "She would, over the course of her ministry, lead over 1500 people to the waters of baptism, convert denominational preachers, and fight a battle for her own integrity."[104]

Many of the Church of Christ leaders in the late 1800s opposed women's suffrage, yet even so, a number of women from the Church of Christ became involved in the campaign to allow voting for women. These women felt that if they could vote, they could do away with the saloons, where much evil occurred. Respected church leader E.W. Herndon, a friend of David Lipscomb (Lipscomb was another key Restoration Movement leader), said, "Voting women violated the scriptural principle of wives being submissive to their husbands." He added, "If the saloons cannot be destroyed except by woman's suffrage, let the saloons stay."[105]

There was some debate in the church over the woman's role. Around the same time (1888), in response to an article that claimed women could teach in private settings but not public ones, Silena Holman, an elder's wife, wrote to a popular Restoration publication, *The Gospel Advocate*:

> Suppose a dozen men and women were in my parlor and I talked to them of the Gospel and exhorted them to obey it, exactly how many men would have to be added to the number to make my talk and exhortation a public and not a private one?[106]

These types of questions led to division over "Sunday school" and whether it was a part of public worship. Some felt it was and did not permit women to teach. Some felt it was not and allowed women to teach men and women if they had expertise on the subject. A few churches allowed women to teach and preach in the assembly, believing that Paul's regulations were cultural and temporary.

Silena engaged this same publication to address a woman's right to exegete and share insights from scriptures during Bible studies. Her comments were met with criticism and ridicule.[107]

The woman's role came to a head in 1892 when both the men's and women's missionary societies decided to hold a joint (coed) convention in Nashville, Tennessee. Nashville, home to Restoration leader David Lipscomb, was the center of the Southern, conservative side of the Restoration Movement. Lipscomb perceived the coed convention as an attempt from the liberal side to take over. He criticized the female attendees, asserting that this "New Womanhood" prostituted the values of "True Womanhood." Furthermore, according to Fred A. Bailey, writing in his essay "The Cult of True Womanhood and the Disciple Path to Women Preaching," Lipscomb "warned his Christian sisters that 'women in pants,' on the rostrum [podium] or managing conventions not only disobey Paul's commands for silence but are also in danger of 'eternal death' in spite of all their 'tender, tearful, heartfelt talks.'"[108]

As we have seen, church and cultural views on the woman's role have gone back and forth again and again. Sadly, views on the role of women have often caused division, including church splits and separations.

When We Focus on the Arrows

Over time, growth in Restoration churches began to wane. Children of members often wandered away from the faith as churches began polishing their arrows of rules and regulations rather than aiming those arrows toward the goal of Christlike love. Whenever this happens, the church slides off the hill and the light grows dim.

> "You are the light of the world. A city on a hill cannot be hidden. Neither do people light a lamp and put it under a bowl. Instead they put it on its stand, and it gives light to everyone in the house. In the same way, let your light shine before men, that they may see your good deeds and praise your Father in heaven." (Matthew 5:14–16 NIV 1984)

And here our ride through history ends, and out we step into the present day. As we step off our ride may we sing, "It's the Lord's world after all, it's our great God's world." May we stand together on the hill, in full view, and let our light shine before the world as we work together, side by side, for the glory of God.

Appendix C

New Wineskins Retreat: A Powerful Example of Inclusion

The following example of partnership is taken from the Foreword by Jerry Taylor, "Jeanene Showed Up and God Showed Out," in Bound and Determined: Christian Men and Women in Partnership *by Jeanene Reese, professor at Abilene Christian University.*

The 2006 New Wineskins Retreat in Malibu, California, was an unforgettable experience. The retreat is an annual gathering of primarily African American ministers and church leaders. It seeks to provide a healthy environment conducive for growth, refreshment, and healing among leaders who are discouraged by an often restrictive religious system.

As we planned the Malibu retreat, it dawned on me that in all of my years of hearing the debate over the role of women in the church, I had never seen women invited to actively participate in the discussion, not to mention lead it. Typically men discussed women's leadership roles while the women sat passively and quietly. In every sense, we failed to partner with our sisters in Christ in this important discussion. As I confronted this realization, I began to see clearly that Christian partnership between men and women was a moral issue.

How could we men have a discussion about women without providing a platform for them to speak in their own voices concerning issues that impact them the most? It would be unthinkable in America today, or at least it should be, to have a discussion about the involvement of African Americans in the life of the church without providing a space for African Americans to speak in their own voices. So it should be for women.

Watching from this insight, I suggested to the planning committee that we conduct the discussion a bit differently than we had approached it in the past. Instead of asking only males to lead the discussion, we would ask all women to be the main presenters and tell us what they thought we most needed to hear. The planning committee readily accepted the idea.

When we started thinking of women who could bring profound insights and brilliant scholarship to the subject, Jeanene Reese's name was among the first we considered. I knew we were on the right track in seeking her participation. I have been fortunate over the years to observe how she consistently displays outstanding leadership and collegiality with grace and strength as a female faculty member in an overwhelmingly male department. The other male faculty and I have benefited personally, spiritually, and professionally as a result of Jeanene's effective mentoring and encouragement.

On that historic day in Malibu, Jeanene stood with three other powerful women of God to courageously address a mostly male audience. As Jeanene spoke in a strong but non-accusatory fashion, it seemed to me that the men discerned her genuine spirit of partnership and solidarity with them. It was special to witness Jeanene's powerful presentation impacting African American men in such a profound way. I think one of the reasons this audience was able to connect with Jeanene as a woman is that African American men are quite familiar with the painful effects of their own marginalization in a majority white society.

Jeanene delivered a memorable message on that occasion, one that had a lasting influence on all those present. As she spoke, it became evident to me that something extraordinary was unfolding in the dynamic exchange between Jeanene and the audience. There seemed to be an electrical current running throughout her presentation that ignited what is known in the Black Church tradition as the "call and response." I had observed this rhythmic give-and-take between the speaker and the audience in the Black Church all of my life. This, however, was the first time I witnessed a call and response taking place between a white female speaker and a predominately black male audience.

I asked myself the question, how could such a powerful moment like this happen? It dawned on me that Jeanene's God-given approach made it possible. She came across as a colleague and not as a competitor. She spoke as an equal and not as an inferior. I noticed the complete absence of fear, judgment, and condemnation in her voice as she expressed her point of view. It was clear that she felt she was in a safe place, among friends who desperately wanted and needed to hear what she had to say on an extremely important subject. It was as if Jeanene's soul transcended her personality as it became increasingly clear that God was doing something uniquely special with her.

In that sacred moment, she became owned by the Word and, therefore, she became "our" speaker. As she spoke with passion, her words inspired life into the broken places within us as men, primarily, and also as African Americans. The spoken Word made it impossible for us to refrain from loudly shouting "yes" to the truth she so effectively proclaimed. We collectively sensed that God was using Jeanene as a mouthpiece for righteousness and truth at such a historic moment.

This holy happening, this sacred occurrence, this major moment in time mediated through a woman of God motivated men of God to stand on their feet in enthusiastic celebration with their voices raised in unfettered joy. I believe that it was at this moment that it became crystal clear to the mainly male audience that the Word of Life still finds free course through all God's children., regardless of gender.

Joseph and Zachariah, the earthly fathers of Jesus and John the Baptist, were blessed to witness the giving of new life through a woman as God's instrument, and in the interchange at this retreat and ever afterward, so were we.[109]

Endnotes

Introduction

[1] Jeanene Reese, *Bound & Determined: Christian Men and Women in Partnership* (Abilene: Leafwood, 2010), 100–101.

Chapter 1

[2] Gordon Ferguson, *The Heart Set Free* (Billerica: Illumination Publishers, 2001), 64.

[3] Some scholars use the word "hermeneutics" to include exegesis **plus** contemporary application. Both exegesis and application involve us being involved in the hermeneutical circle, which is why some put them under one heading as "hermeneutics."

[4] A helpful look at different styles of Biblical writing is found in the first two chapters of Douglas Jacoby's book, *What's the Truth about Heaven and Hell?* (Available at www.ipibooks.com.)

[5] Near the end of his life on earth, Jesus prayed for complete unity for his disciples (John 17:6–23); in its early days, the church Jesus had died to build portrayed a spirit of unity as no one called anything their own (Acts 2:44–47).

[6] Timeless principles applicable to employer/employee relationships could possibly be derived from the scriptures on slavery.

[7] This look at slavery (as an example of the need to define our hermeneutic) is from a conversation with Michael Burns, historian, author, and teacher.

[8] William J. Webb, Slaves, *Women & Homosexuals: Exploring the Hermeneutics of Cultural Analysis* (Downers Grove: InterVarsity Press, 2001), 56–57. Webb uses distinct criteria to expose the cultural nature of Paul's teachings on slavery and women, while using the same criteria to show the timeless principle in the Scriptures' prohibition of homosexual behavior.

Chapter 2

[9] Thankfully, since then the culture for women has greatly changed—in the church and in the world. I am grateful for all the people who have worked over the years to help women become more valued in the church. I am grateful for the women who went before me in my country, fighting long and hard for privileges I now

enjoy, including the rights to vote and to serve in public office. And I am thankful for those who have worked (and continue to work) toward equal pay for women. Women in numerous other countries still don't have some of the privileges I enjoy, but even so, my culture still needs to make significant progress. I write these pages during a time when male entertainment leaders, news anchors, and political leaders are finally being called to account for years of sexual harassment and lewd behavior toward women in the workplace.

[10] Scot McKnight, *The Blue Parakeet: Rethinking How You Read the Bible* (Grand Rapids: Zondervan, 2008), 189.

[11] R. Laird Harris, Gleson L. Archer Jr. and Bruce Waltke, eds, *Theological Wordbook of the Old Testament* (Chicago: Moody Press, 1980), 2:768.

[12] Carolyn Custis James, *Half the Church: Recapturing God's Global Vision for Women* (Grand Rapids: Zondervan, 2010), 100-101.

[13] U.S. Census Bureau; American Community Survey, 2009, Summary Tables; generated using FactFinder; see http://factfinder.census.gov, cited in Carolyn Custis James, *Half the Church: Recapturing God's Global Vision for Women* (Grand Rapids: Zondervan, 2010), 102–103.

[14] This information about the meaning of *ezer kenegdo* in the Old Testament is the refinement of several email exchanges with congregational teachers in the Midwest and a result of conversations with Phil Lasarsky, current participant in the Spertus Institute for Jewish Learning, MAJS program, and with Spertus Faculty and The Asher Library of Judaic Studies.

[15] Carolyn Custis James, *Half the Church: Recapturing God's Global Vision for Women* (Grand Rapids: Zondervan, 2010), 106, 112, 115.

[16] Kenneth Bailey, *Jesus Through Middle Eastern Eyes: Cultural Studies in the Gospels* (Downers Grove: InterVarsity Press, 2008), 189–90.

[17] Bailey, 194-195.

[18] Bailey, 193.

Chapter 3

[19] Table V, http://www.historyguide.org/ancient/12tables.html.

[20] William Barclay, *The New Daily Study Bible: The Letters to Timothy, Titus, and Philemon* (Louisville: Westminster John Knox Press, 2003), 75.

[21] The origin of this prayer is found in the Tosefta to Berakhot 6:16. The Tosefta is a compilation of the Jewish oral law from the late 2nd century, the period of the Mishnah.

[22] 24 Babylonian Talmud, GiṬṬ in 90a-b.

[23] Alfred Edersheim, *Sketches of Jewish Social Life in the Days of Christ* (Grand Rapids: Eerdmans, 1970 reprint of 1876 edition),146), Edersheim notes Rabbinic "exposition" of Genesis 2:21-22.

[24] Lynn H. Cohick, *Women in the World of the Earliest Christians: Illuminating Ancient Ways of Life* (Grand Rapids: Baker Academics, 2009), 324.

[25] John T. Bristow, *What Paul Really Said About Women: The Apostle's Liberating Views on Equality in Marriage, Leadership, and Love* (San Francisco: Harper Collins, 2011, location 96, Kindle.

Chapter 4

[26] Bruce, W. Winter, *Roman Wives, Roman Widows: The Appearance of New Women and the Pauline Communities* (Grand Rapids: Wm. B. Eerdmans, 2003), locations 339–341, Kindle.

[27] Lynn H. Cohick, *Women in the World of the Earliest Christians: Illuminating Ancient Ways of Life* (Grand Rapids: Baker Academic, 2009), 72, 73, 78.

[28] While I have used other sources, much information concerning "new women" is from Bruce Winters. His work is commended by many scholars, such as in this review by the late renowned scholar I. Howard Marshall. https://www.scribd.com/document/324821156/Review-Winter-Bruce-Roman-Wives-Roman-Widows

Chapter 5

[29] Winter, locations 528-532, Kindle.

[30] Carl Spain, *The Letters of Paul to Timothy and Titus* (Austin: R.B. Sweet Co., 1970) 21–22.

[31] Patricia Monaghan, *Encyclopedia of Goddesses and Heroines,* Santa Barbara, CA: Greenwood, 2010, accessed March 1, 2019, http://eres.regent.edu:2048/login?url=http://search.ebscohost.com/login.aspx?direct=true&db=nlebk&AN=323500&site=ehost-live.

Chapter 6

[32] Bruce W. Winter, *Roman Wives, Roman Widows: The Appearance of New Women and the Pauline Communities* (Grand Rapids: Wm. B. Eerdmans, 2003), location 1011, Kindle.

[33] Andreas Krotenberger, and Thomas Schreiner, *Women in the Church: An Interpretation and Application of 1 Timothy 2:9–15, 3rd Edition* (Wheaton: Crossway, 2016), 47.

[34] Clinton E. Arnold, General Editor, *Zondervan Illustrated Bible Backgrounds Commentary* (Grand Rapids: Zondervan, 2002), 456.

[35] Clinton E. Arnold, *Exegetical Commentary on the New Testament* (Grand Rapids: Zondervan, 2010), 374–375.

[36] Richard Lattimore, Illinois *Studies In Language And Literature, V28, No. 1–2*, (Whitefish: Literary Licensing LLC, 2012), 293.

[37] Manfred T. Brauch, *Hard Sayings of Paul* (Downers Grove: Intervarsity Press, 1989), 259.

[38] Bruce W. Winter, *Roman Wives, Roman Widows: The Appearance of New Women and the Pauline Communities* (Grand Rapids: Wm. B. Eerdmans, 2003), locations 944–949, 987, Kindle.

[39] Paul Zanker, *The Power of Images in the Age of Augustus* (Ann Arbor: University of Michigan Press, 1990), 165.

[40] Sir William Ramsay, *The Cities of St. Paul; Their Influence on His Life and Thought*, (New York; A.C. Armstrong and ; London: Hodder and Stoughton, 1908), 204-205.

[41] https://www.sbl-site.org/publications/article.aspx?ArticleId=271.

[42] Winter, location 1031–1035, Kindle.

[43] Mark Stansbury-O'Donnell, *Vase Painting, Gender, and Social Identity in Archaic Athens* (Cambridge: Cambridge University Press, 2006), 219.

[44] Winter, location 1101–1104, Kindle.

[45] www.blueletterbible.orgsearchsearchcfm?Criteria=%22of+the+angels%22&t=NIV#s=s_faqs_1

[46] Winter, locations, 1074–1079, Kindle.

Chapter 7

[47] Manfred Brauch, *Hard Sayings of Paul* (Downers Grove: InterVarsity Press, 1989), 264.

[48] Paul was inspired by the Holy Spirit as he penned these letters. My focus on his training as a rabbi and Pharisee is to show that he would have been familiar with and influenced by rabbinic teaching methods (such as the ones concerning creation order).

[49] F. F. Bruce, Manfred T. Brauch, Peter Davids, and Walter Kaiser Jr., *Hard Sayings of the Bible* (Downers Grove: InterVarsity Press, 1996), 669–670.

[50] Bruce K. Waltke, editor D.A. Carson, *The Enduring Authority of the Christian Scriptures*, (Grand Rapids: Eerdmans, 2016), 570.

[51] This belief that women are more easily deceived does not square with current empirical data which tells us that in our culture gullibility is primarily related to age, experience, intelligence, education, and personality—and has nothing to do with gender. William J. Webb, *Slaves, Women & Homosexuals: Exploring the Hermeneutics of Cultural Analysis*, (Downers Grove: InterVarsity Press, 2001), 113. Would the data have been different if collected in Paul's day? It would seem likely, as women in patriarchal societies generally married young (as teens), weren't permitted the experiences available to men, and did not have the same educational opportunities.

[52] Manfred T Brauch, Hard Sayings of Paul (Downers Grove: InterVarsity Press, 1989), 262.

[53] Brauch, 263.

[54] Brauch, 263.

[55] Sarah Sumner, *Men and Women in the Church:Building Consensus on Christian Leadership*, (Downers Grove: Inter-Varsity Press, 2003), 259-261.

Chapter 8

[56] See definitions for ἡσυχάζω and ἡσυχία, ας, ἡ found in Arndt, W., Danker, F. W., Bauer, W., & Gingrich, F. W. (2000). *A Greek-English Lexicon of the New Testament and Other Early Christian Literature*, 3rd ed, (Chicago: University of Chicago Press), 440.

[57] https://www.blueletterbible.org/niv/1th/4/11/t_conc_1115011

[58] https://www.blueletterbible.org/niv/luk/23/56/t_conc_996056

[59] https://www.blueletterbible.org/niv/2th/3/12/t_conc_1119012

[60] https://www.blueletterbible.org/niv/1ti/2/12/t_conc_1121012

[61] As defined in Vine's Expository Dictionary

[62] As found in Thayer's Greek Lexicon, Electronic Database, Biblesoft, 2011.

[63] https://margmowczko.com/authentein-1-timothy2_12/

[64] David Scholer, essay, *"Women in Ministry—A Biblical Basis for Equal Partnership,"* Fuller Theological Seminary, http://fuller.edu/womeninministry/

[65] www.blueletterbible.org/niv/1co/14/26/t_conc_1076034

[66] Browning, W. R. F.Browning, "glossolalia." *In A Dictionary of the Bible* (Oxford University Press, 2009), accessed March 4, 2019, http://www.oxfordreference.com.ezproxy.regent.edu:2048/view/10.1093/acref/9780199543984.001.0001/acref-9780199543984-e-764.

[67] www.blueletterbible.org/niv/1co/14/26/t_conc_1076034

[68] "Women in Ministry, 1 Cor. 14:34-35," https://www.fuller.edu/womeninministry/

[69] Dan Doriani, *Women and Ministry: What the Bible Teaches* (Wheaton: Crossway Books, 2003), 82.

[70] Craig Keener, Paul, *Women, and Wives: Marriage and Women's Ministry in the Letters of Paul* (Peabody: Hendrickson Publishers, 2009), 72, 83.

Chapter 9

[71] The debate is recorded in a highly abbreviated form in m. Git. 9.10: cf. Sifre Deut. 269; y. Git. 50a; b. Git. 90a; Sota 16b-c.

[72] https://www.douglasjacoby.com/wp-content/uploads/Instone-Brewer-on-Divorce-Remarriage-1.pdf has a summary of his views.

[73] Mary Lefkowitz and Maureen Fant, *Women's Life in Greece and Rome: A Source Book in Translation*, 2nd edition (Baltimore: John Hopkins University Press, 1992), 187.

[74] Tim Muehlhoff and Todd Lewis, *Authentic Communication: Christian Speech Engaging Culture* (Downers Grove: InterVarsity Press, 2010), 206.

[75] Lynn H. Cohick, *Women in the World of the Earliest Christians: Illuminating Ancient Ways of Life*, (Grand Rapids: Baker Academic, 2009), 67.

[76] Aristotle, *Pol.* 1.12, (1259a.35-1259h.9).

[77] Soranus, *Gyn.* 3.3, Translation in Soranus' Gynecology, trans. O.Temkin (Baltimore: Johns Hopkins University Press, 1991), 129.

[78] Plutarch, Mor. 748e-771e; 138a-146a (=Conj. praec.). Cited in Lynn H. Cohick, *Women in the World of the Earliest Christians: Illuminating Ancient Ways of Life*, (Grand

Rapids: Baker Academic, 2009), 71.

[79] William J. Webb, *Slaves, Women & Homosexuals: Exploring the Hermeneutics of Cultural Analysis*, (Downers Grove: InterVarsity Press, 2001), 80.

[80] Webb, 79-80.

[81] https://www.cbeinternational.org/resources/article/priscilla-papers/meta-study-debate-over-meaning-%E2%80%9Chead%E2%80%9D-kephal%C4%93-paul%E2%80%99s-writings

[82] Alice Mathews, *Gender Roles and the People of God: Rethinking What We Were Taught about Men and Women in the Church*, (Grand Rapids: Zondervan, 2017), 125–126.

[83] Sarah Sumner, *Men and Women in the Church: Building Consensus on Christian Leadership*, (Downers Grove: Inter-Varsity Press, 2003), 167.

[84] William J. Webb, *Slaves, Women & Homosexuals: Exploring the Hermeneutics of Cultural Analysis*, (Downers Grove: InterVarsity Press, 2001), 108.

Chapter 10

[85] Michelle Lee-Barnewall, *Neither Complementarian nor Egalitarian: A Kingdom Corrective to the Evangelical Gender Debate* (Grand Rapids: Baker Academic, 2016), 173, 177.

Chapter 11

[86] Phoebe was a patron, sister, and minister (διακονος or *diakonos*) who worked closely with Paul and carried his letter to Rome. Letter carriers were not like our modern-day mail carriers. Once they reached the church with the letter, they would both read and expound on it, making sure the intent was clear. Phoebe was likely coached by Paul for how to publicly deliver the message to the church in Rome.

Robin Gallaher Branch, "Female Leadership as Demonstrated by Phoebe: An Interpretation of Paul's Words Introducing Phoebe to the Saints in Rome," *In Die Skriflig* 53, no. 2 (2019), doi:http://dx.doi.org.ezproxy.regent.edu:2048/10.4102/ids.v53i2.2443. http://eres.regent.edu:2048/login?url=https://search-proquest-com.ezproxy.regent.edu/docview/2327805870?accountid=13479.

[87] Scot McKnight, *The Blue Parakeet: Rethinking How You Read the Bible* (Grand Rapids: Zondervan, 2008), 204.

[88] Alan F. Johnson, *How I Changed My Mind about Women in Leadership: Compelling Stories from Prominent Evangelicals* (Grand Rapids: Zondervan, 2010), location 43, Kindle.

Appendix A

[89] Brian J. Dodd. *The Problem with Paul* (Kindle Locations 884–887, 915–916, 943–959). Kindle Edition.

Appendix B

[90] "The Politics of Gender in Early Modern Europe," Kirksville, MO, Sixteenth Century Journal, 1989, 61, cited in Alice Mathews, *Gender Roles and the People of God: Rethinking What We Were Taught About Men and Women in the Church* (Grand Rapids: Zondervan, 2017), 171.

[91] See Thomas Aquinas, Summa Theologica, 1.92.1,ad.1.

[92] Alice Mathews, *Gender Roles and the People of God: Rethinking What We Were Taught about Men and Women in the Church,* (Grand Rapids: Zondervan, 2017), 178-179.

[93] Torjesen, When Women Were Priests, p. 233. Cited in Mathews, Alice, *Gender Roles and the People of God Rethinking What We Were Taught About Men and Women in the Church* (Grand Rapids: Zondervan, 2017), 180.

[94] Julia O'Faolain and Lauro Matines, eds. *Not in God's Image* (New York: Harper, 1973), 247.

[95] Jean Bethke Elshtain, *Kant, Politics, and Persons: The Implications of His Moral Philosophy*, Polity 14.2 (1981); 213.

[96] Marie Jean Antoine Nicolas d Caritat, Marquis de Condorcer, "On the Admission of Women to the Rights of Citizenship" (1790) cited in Mathews, Alice, *Gender Roles and the People of God* (Grand Rapids: Zondervan, 2017).

[97] Ann Douglas, *The Feminization of American Culture* (New York: Avon, 1977), 23–24.

[98] Alice Mathews, *Gender Roles and the People of God: Rethinking What We Were Taught about Men and Women in the Church,* (Grand Rapids: Zondervan, 2017) 197.

[99] Betty DeBerg, *Ungodly Women: Gender and the First Wave of American Fundamentalism* (Minneapolis: Fortress, 1990), 15–16. Cited in Mathews, Alice, *Gender*

Roles and the People of God, 204.

[100] Barbara Berg, *The Remembered Gate* (New York: Oxford University Press, 1978), 109. Cited in *Gender Roles and the People of God* (Grand Rapids: Zondervan, 2017), 205.

[101] Barbara Berg, *The Remembered Gate* (New York: Oxford University Press, 1978), 109. Cited in Alice Mathews, *Gender Roles and the People of God: Rethinking What We Were Taught about Men and Women in the Church* (Grand Rapids: Zondervan, 2017), 205.

[102] Isaac Jones, *The Reformation in Tennessee,* cited by JM Grant in "A Sketch of the Reformation in Tennessee," manuscript, Center for Restoration Studies, ACU, 55.

[103] "Church Organization #2" MH 1853, p. 185)
(Organization #3, MH 1853, p. 247)

[104] http://stonedcampbelldisciple.com/2016/02/03/clara-celestia-hale-babcock-1850-1924-first-ordained-gospel-preacher. See this article for more information on women during this time period.

[105] E.W. Herndon, "Women's Suffrage," *Christian Quarterly Review 7* (October 1888), 608; cited from Fred A Baily, "The Status of Women in the Disciples of Christ Movement, 1865–1900" PhD dissertation University of Tennessee, 1979, 229–30.

[106] Silena Holman, "Let Your Women Keep Silent," GA 30, August 1, 1888, 8; cited from Allen, *Distant Voices,* 128–129.

[107] http://stonedcampbelldisciple.com/2016/01/28/silena-moore-holman/

[108] Lipscomb, "An Unjust Charge," GA 34, (December 1, 1892: 756; quoted from Fred A. Bailey, "The Disciples Path," 514 and cited in a paper by Bill Grasham, "The Role of Women in the American Restoration Movement" (Center for Continuing Education with copyright pending).

Appendix C

[109] Jeanene Reese, *Bound & Determined: Christian Men and Women in Partnership,* (Abilene, Leafwood Press, 2010), foreword by Dr. Jerry Taylor.

Bibliography

Aquinas, Thomas, "Summa Theologica", 1.92.1, ad. 1

Arndt, W., Danker, F.W., Bauer, W. and Gingrich, F., *A Greek-English Lexicon of the New Testament and Other Early Christian Literature, 3rd Edition,* Chicago: University of Chicago Press, 2000.

Arnold, Clinton. *Exegetical Commentary on the New Testament.* Grand Rapids: Zondervan, 2010.

Arnold, Clinton, general editor. *Zondervan Illustrated Bible Backgrounds Commentary.* Grand Rapid.s: Zondervan, 2002.

Aristotle, *Pol.* 1.12, 1259a.35-1259h.9.

Bailey, Kenneth. *Jesus Through Middle Eastern Eyes: Cultural Studies in the Gospels.* Downers Grove: InterVarsity Press, 2008.

Baily, Fred, "The Status of Women in the Disciples of Christ Movement, 1865-1900", Ph.D dissertation University of Tennessee, 1979.

Barclay, William. *The Letters to Galatians and Ephesians.* Philadelphia: Westminster Press, 1976.

Barclay, William. *The Letters to the Corinthians, revised edition.* Philadelphia: Westminster Press, 1975.

Barclay, William. *The New Daily Study Bible: The Letters to Timothy, Titus, and Philemon.* Louisville: Westminster John Knox Press, 2003.

Beck, James R., general editor, *Two Views on Women and Ministry.* Grand Rapids: Zondervan, 2005.

Berg, Barbara. *The Remembered Gate.* New York: Oxford University Press, 1978.

Branch, Robin Gallaher. "Female Leadership as Demonstrated by Phoebe: An Interpretation of Paul's Words Introducing Phoebe to the Saints in Rome." *In Die Skriflig* 53, no. 2 (2019). doi:http://dx.doi.org.ezproxy.regent.edu:2048/10.4102/ids.v53i2.2443. http://eres.regent.edu:2048/login?url=https://search-proquest-com.ezproxy.regent.edu/docview/2327805870?accountid=13479.

Brauch, Manfred. *Hard Sayings of Paul*. Downers Grove: InterVarsity Press, 1989.

Bristow, John. *What Paul Really Said About Women: The Apostle's Liberating Views on Equality in Marriage, Leadership, and Love*. New York: Harper Collins, 1988.

Bruce, F.F., Brauch, Manfred, Davids, Peter H., Kaiser, Walter Jr., *Hard Sayings of the Bible*. Downers Grove: InterVarsity, 1996.

Cohick, Lynn H., PhD. *Women in the World of the Earliest Christians: Illuminating Ancient Ways of Life*. Grand Rapids: Baker Academics, 2009.

DeBerg, Betty. *Ungodly Women: Gender and the First Wave of American Fundamentalism*. Minneapolis: Fortress, 1990.

D'Este, Sorita, Artemis: *Virgin Goddess of the Sun & Moon*. London: Avalonia, 2005.

Dodd, Brian J. *The Problem with Paul*. Downers Grove: InterVarsity, 1996.

Doriani, Dan. *Women and Ministry: What the Bible Teaches*. Wheaton: Crossway, 2003.

Douglas, Ann. *The Feminization of American Culture*. New York: Avon, 1977.

Elshtain, Jean Bethke, Kant, *Politics and Persons: The Implications of His Moral Philosophy*, Polity 14.2, 1981

Fee, Gordon. *The First Epistle to the Corinthians, Revised Edition*. Grand Rapids: Wm. B. Eerdmans, 2014.

Ferguson, Gordon. *The Heart Set Free*. Billerica: DPI, 2001.

Grasham, Bill. *The Role of Women in the American Restoration Movement.* PDF.

Gruyter, Walter. (Translated by Helen and Mervyn Richardson), *Women in the Ancient Near* East. Boston/Berlin: Walter de Gruyter Inc. 2016.

Highfield, Ron. *Four Views on Women and Church Leadership: Should Bible Believing* (Evangelical) Churches Appoint Women Preachers, Pastors, Elders, and Bishops? Los Angeles: Keledei, 2017.

Holman, Silena, "Let Your Women Keep Silent," *Gospel Advocate 30,* August 1, 1888.

Hughes, Richard. *Reviving the Ancient Faith: The Story of Churches of Christ in America.* Grand Rapids: Wm. B. Eerdmans, 1996.

Hyatt, Susan C. *In the Spirit We're Equal: The Spirit, the Bible, & Women, A Revival Perspective.* Grapevine: Hayatt, 1998.

International Church of Christ Teachers Task Force. *The Bible and Gender.* Spring, TX: Illumination Publishers, 2020.

James, Carolyn Custis. *Half the Church: Recapturing God's Global Vision for Women.* Grand Rapids: Zondervan, 2010.

Johnson, Alan. *How I Changed My Mind about Women in Leadership: Compelling Stories from Prominent Evangelicals.* Grand Rapids: Zondervan, 2010.

Jones, Isaac, *The Reformation in Tennessee,* cited by J.M. Grant in "A Sketch of the Reformation in Tennessee manuscript", Center for Restoration Studies, ACU, 55.

Keener, Craig. Paul, *Women, and Wives: Marriage and Women's Ministry in the Letters of Paul.,* Peabody: Hendrickson, 2009.

Kröstenberger, Andreas, and Schreiner, Thomas. *Women in the Church: An Interpretation and Application of 1 Timothy 2:9-15, 3rd Edition.* Wheaton: Crossway, 2016.

Laird, Harris R., Archer, Gleson L. Jr., and Waltke, Bruce. *Theological Wordbook of the Old Testament.* Chicago: Moody, 1980.

Lee-Barnewall, Michelle. *Neither Complementarian nor Egalitarian: A Kingdom Corrective to the Evangelical Gender Debate*. Grand Rapids: Baker Academics, 2016.

Lattimore, Richard, "Illinois Studies in Language and Literature" Vol. 28, No. 1-2, Whitefish: Literary Licensing LLC, 2012.

Lefkowitz, Mary, and Fant, Maureen. *Women's Life in Greece and Rome: A Source Book in Translation, 2nd Edition*. Baltimore: John Hopkins University Press, 1992.

Marshall, Howard, https://www.scribd.com/document/324821156/Review-Winter-Bruce-Roman-Wives-Roman-Widows.

Mathews, Alice. *Gender Roles and the People of God: Rethinking What We Were Taught about Men and Women in the Church*. New York: Harper Collins, 2017.

McKnight, Scot. *The Blue Parakeet: Rethinking How You Read the Bible*. Grand Rapids: Zondervan, 2008.

Monaghan, Patricia, *Encyclopedia of Goddesses and Heroines*. Santa Barbara: Greenwood, 2010.

Muelhoff, Tim and Lewis, Todd. *Authentic Communication: Christian Speech Engaging Culture*. Downers Grove: InterVarsity, 2010.

O'Faolain and Matines, Lauro, eds. *Not in God's Image*. New York: Harper, 1973.

Osburn, Carroll. *Essays on Women in Earliest Christianity Volumes 1 and 2*. Eugene: Wipf and Stock, 1993.

Pierce, Ronald W. Ph.D, Groothuis, Rebecca Merrill, Fee, Gordon D. Ph.D, *Discovering Biblical Equality:Complementary Without Hierarchy*. Downers Grove: InterVarsity, 2005.

Piper, John and Grudem, Wayne. *Biblical Manhood and Womanhood: A Response to Evangelical Feminism*. Wheaton: Crossway, 2006.

Powell, Mark Allan, *Introducing the New Testament: A Historical, Literary, and Theological Survey*, Grand Rapids: Baker Academics, 2018.

Ramsay, Sir William, *The Cities of St. Paul: Their Influence on His Life and Thought*, London: Hodder and Stoughton, 1908.

Reese, Jeanene, *Bound & Determined: Christian Men and Women in Partnership*. Abilene: Leafwood, 2010.

Richards, E. Randolph, and O'Brien J. *Misreading Scripture With Western Eyes: Removing Cultural Blinders to Better Understand the Bible*. Downers Grove: InterVarsity, 2012.

Richards, E. Randolph, and O'Brien J. *Paul Behaving Badly*, Downers Grove: InterVarsity, 2016.

Scholer, David. *Essay on Women in Ministry: A Biblical Basis for Equal Partnership*, Fuller Theological Seminary.

Soranus, *Gyn*. 3.3, "Translation in Soranus' Gynecology, trans. O. Temkin, Baltimore: John Hopkins University Press, 1991.

Spain, Carl. *The Letters of Paul to Timothy and Titus*, Austin: R.B. Sweet, 1970.

Stansbury-O'Donell, Mark. *Vase Painting, Gender, and Social Identity in Archaic Athens*, Cambridge: Cambridge University Press, 2006.

Sumner, Sarah, *Men and Women in the Church*, Downers Grove: InterVarsityPress, 2003

Vine, W.E., Unger, Merrill, and White, William Jr. *Vine's Expository Dictionary*, Nashville: Thomas Nelson, 1996 (Kindle Edition).

Waltke, Bruce, *An Old Testament Theology*. Grand Rapids: Zondervan, 2007.

Webb, William J. *Slaves, Women, & Homosexuals: Exploring the Hermeneutics Of Cultural Analysis*. Downers Grove: InterVarsity, 2001.

Westfall, Cynthia Long, *Paul and Gender: Reclaiming the Apostle's Vision for Men and Women in Christ*, Grand Rapids: Baker Academic, 2016.

Winter, Bruce W. *Roman Wives, Roman Widows: The Appearance of New Women and the Pauline Communities,* Downers Grove: InterVarsity, 2001.

Witherington, Ben III. *Women and the Genesis of Christianity,* New York: Cambridge University Press, 1995.

Zanker, Paul. *The Power of Images in the Age of Augustus,* Ann Arbor: University of Michigan Press, 1990.

Books by Jeanie Shaw

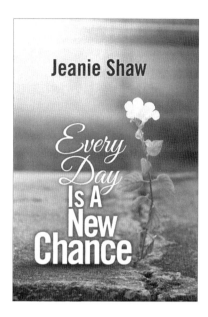
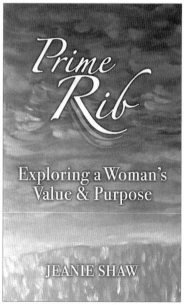

These and more available at
www.ipibooks.com

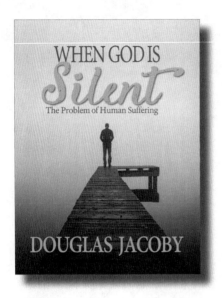
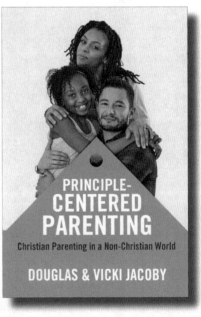

Available at www.ipibooks.com

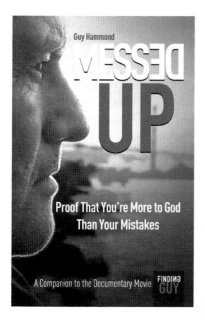

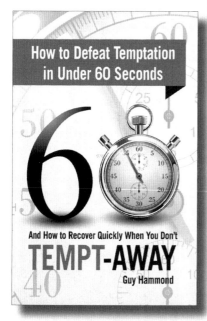

Available at www.ipibooks.com

Books for Christian Growth from Illumination Publishers

Apologetics
Compelling Evidence for God and the Bible—Truth in an Age of Doubt, by Douglas Jacoby.
Field Manual for Christian Apologetics, by John M. Oakes.
Is There A God—Questions and Answers about Science and the Bible, by John M. Oakes.
Mormonism—What Do the Evidence and Testimony Reveal?, by John M. Oakes.
Reasons For Belief–A Handbook of Christian Evidence, by John M. Oakes.
That You May Believe—Reflections on Science and Jesus, by John Oakes/David Eastman.
The Resurrection: A Historical Analysis, by C. Foster Stanback.
When God Is Silent—The Problem of Human Suffering, by Douglas Jacoby.

Bible Basics
A Disciple's Handbook—Third Edition, Tom A. Jones, Editor.
A Quick Overview of the Bible, by Douglas Jacoby.
Be Still, My Soul—A Practical Guide to a Deeper Relationship with God, by Sam Laing.
From Shadow to Reality—Relationship of the Old & New Testament, by John M. Oakes.
Getting the Most from the Bible, Second Edition, by G. Steve Kinnard.
Letters to New Disciples—Practical Advice for New Followers of Jesus, by Tom A. Jones.
The Baptized Life—The Lifelong Meaning of Immersion into Christ, by Tom A. Jones.
The Lion Never Sleeps—Preparing Those You Love for Satans Attacks, by Mike Taliaferro.
The New Christian's Field Guide, Joseph Dindinger, Editor.
Thirty Days at the Foot of the Cross, Tom and Sheila Jones, Editors.

Christian Living
According to Your Faith—The Awesome Power of Belief in God, by Richard Alawaye.
But What About Your Anger—A Biblical Guide to Managing Your Anger, by Lee Boger.
Caring Beyond the Margins—Understanding Homosexuality, by Guy Hammond.
Golden Rule Membership—What God Expects of Every Disciple, by John M. Oakes.
How to Defeat Temptation in Under 60 Seconds, by Guy Hammond.
Jesus and the Poor—Embracing the Ministry of Jesus, by G. Steve Kinnard.
How to Be a Missionary in Your Hometown, by Joel Nagel.
Like a Tree Planted by Streams of Water—Personal Spiritual Growth, G. Steve Kinnard.
Love One Another—Importance & Power of Christian Relationships, by Gordon Ferguson.
One Another—Transformational Relationships, by Tom A. Jones and Steve Brown.
Prepared to Answer—Restoring Truth in An Age of Relativism, by Gordon Ferguson.
Repentance—A Cosmic Shift of Mind & Heart, by Edward J. Anton.
Strong in the Grace—Reclaiming the Heart of the Gospel, by Tom A. Jones.
The Guilty Soul's Guide to Grace—Freedom in Christ, by Sam Laing.
The Power of Discipling, by Gordon Ferguson.
The Prideful Soul's Guide to Humility, by Tom A. Jones and Michael Fontenot.
The Way of the Heart—Spiritual Living in a Legalistic World, by G. Steve Kinnard.
The Way of the Heart of Jesus—Prayer, Fasting, Bible Study, by G. Steve Kinnard.
Till the Nets Are Full—An Evangelism Handbook for the 21st Century, by Douglas Jacoby.
Walking the Way of the Heart—Lessons for Spiritual Living, by G. Steve Kinnard.
When God is Silent—The Problem of Human Suffering, by Douglas Jacoby.
Values and Habits of Spiritual Growth, by Bryan Gray.

All these and more available at www.ipibooks.com

Deeper Study

A Women's Ministry Handbook, by Jennifer Lambert and Kay McKean.
After The Storm—Hope & Healing From Ezra—Nehemiah, by Rolan Dia Monje.
Aliens and Strangers—The Life and Letters of Peter, by Brett Kreider.
Crossing the Line: Culture, Race, and Kingdom, by Michael Burns.
Daniel—Prophet to the Nations, by John M. Oakes.
Exodus—Making Israel's Journey Your Own, by Rolan Dia Monje.
Exodus—Night of Redemption, by Douglas Jacoby.
Finish Strong—The Message of Haggai, Zechariah, and Malachi, by Rolan Dia Monje.
Free Your Mind—40 Days to Greater Peace, Hope, and Joy, by Sam Laing.
In Remembrance of Me—Understanding the Lord's Supper, by Andrew C. Fleming.
In the Middle of It!—Tools to Help Preteen and Young Teens, by Jeff Rorabaugh.
Into the Psalms—Verses for the Heart, Music for the Soul, by Rolan Dia Monje.
King Jesus—A Survey of the Life of Jesus the Messiah, by G. Steve Kinnard.
Jesus Unequaled—An Exposition of Colossians, by G. Steve Kinnard.
Mornings in Matthew, by Tammy Fleming.
Passport to the Land of Enough—Revised Edition, by Joel Nagel.
Prophets I—The Voices of Yahweh, by G. Steve Kinnard.
Prophets II—The Prophets of the Assyrian Period, by G. Steve Kinnard.
Prophets III—The Prophets of the Babylonian and Persion Periods, by G. Steve Kinnard.
Return to Sender—When There's Nowhere Left to God but Home, by Guy Hammond.
Romans—The Heart Set Free, by Gordon Ferguson.
Revelation Revealed—Keys to Unlocking the Mysteries of Revelation, by Gordon Ferguson.
Spiritual Leadership for Women, Jeanie Shaw, Editor.
The Call of the Wise—An Introduction and Index of Proverbs, by G. Steve Kinnard.
The Cross of the Savior—From the Perspective of Jesus..., by Mark Templer.
The Final Act—A Biblical Look at End-Time Prophecy, by G. Steve Kinnard.
The Gospel of Matthew—The Crowning of the King, by G. Steve Kinnard.
The Letters of James, Peter, John, Jude—Life to the Full, by Douglas Jacoby.
The Lion Has Roared—An Exposition of Amos, by Douglas Jacoby.
The Seven People Who Help You to Heaven, by Sam Laing.
The Spirit—Presense & Power, Sense & Nonsense, by Douglas Jacoby.
Thrive—Using Psalms to Help You Flourish, by Douglas Jacoby.
What Happens After We Die?, by Douglas Jacoby.
World Changers—The History of the Church in the Book of Acts, by Gordon Ferguson.

Marriage and Family

A Lifetime of Love—Building and Growing Your Marriage, by Al and Gloria Baird
Building Emotional Intimacy in Your Marriage, by Jeff and Florence Schachinger.
Hot and Holy—God's Plan for Exciting Sexual Intimacy in Marriage, by Sam Laing.
Faith and Finances, by Patrick Blair.
Friends & Lovers—Marriage as God Designed It, by Sam and Geri Laing.
Mighty Man of God—A Return to the Glory of Manhood, by Sam Laing.
Pure the Journey—A Radical Journey to a Pure Heart, by David and Robin Weidner.
Raising Awesome Kids—Being the Great Influence in Your Kids' Lives by Sam and Geri Laing.
Principle-Centered Parenting, by Douglas and Vicki Jacoby.
The Essential 8 Principles of a Growing Christian Marriage, by Sam and Geri Laing.
The Essential 8 Principles of a Strong Family, by Sam and Geri Laing.
Warrior—A Call to Every Man Everywhere, by Sam Laing.

All these and more available at www.ipibooks.com

att

— PODCAST —
Help me Teach the Bible
Nancy Guthrie

www.ipibooks.com